Artifice in the Calm Damages

Artifice in the Calm Damages

identity
flesh
songs of innocence

Andrew Levy

foreword by Tyrone Williams

chax
2021

ISBN 978-1-946104-26-7

Library of Congress Control Number: 2020943170

Chax Press

1517 N Wilmot Rd n. 264

Tucson Arizona 85712-4410

Chax Press books are supported in part by individual donors and by sales of the books. Please visit https://chax.org/membership-support/ if you would like to contribute to our mission to make an impact on literature and culture of our time.

Frontispiece by Sadie Levy, "Practice Lines" (2019).

Some of us who have already begun to break the silence of the night have found that the calling to speak is often a vocation of agony, but we must speak. We must speak with all the humility that is appropriate to our limited vision, but we must speak.
~ Martin Luther King, Jr.

When we are where we shall exercise
Our mysterious craft, we seem wonderfully wise,
Our terms are so scholarly and so strange.
I blow the fire until my heart faints.
Why should I tell each proportion
Of the things that we work upon…
~ Geoffrey Chaucer, "The Canon's Yeoman's Tale"
The CanterburyTales

I am at home in the entire world, where there are clouds and birds and human tears.
~ Rosa Luxemburg

to Sally, Gita, and Sadie

who teach me how to look at the world

to America

whatever that is

FOREWORD

"The poem is first of all your concept of the poem." Fair warning to the general reader, for with the large declamations of *Artifice In The Calm Damages*, Andrew Levy lays claim to Whitman's burden ("I was on the street in Manhattan, my ears to the ground"), if not title, sorting through the smoldering ruins of cultural meanings, social communication and political community. Framed by the Bomb and its children, the baby boomers ("The land of the free/ is a tiny child trying to climb onto the rim of a well"), on the one hand, and the Babyface Nelsons of adult adolescence ("No baby shall see the end. Its diaper is of fire/ and its gun is a lead flame.") on the other, *Artifice In the Calm Damages* is an argument for a cultural and social revolution, its political and economic cognates having come up short ("This is why facts are insufficient remedy for dislodging/ bullets from those who have weakly held positions"). But Levy, wary of the one-upmanship of cultural *productivity* ("My work? Whatever you want here, I want more than you want"), concedes nothing, least of all the political and economic spheres. Levy rolls the dice, taking the chance that artifice ("just text instead of/ Justice") might be something more than "A calm within damage so extensive that we no longer know it/ To be anything other than a part from ourselves[.]" Refusing the bromides "Cascading through all common and private goods," Levy deploys the imperative voice, heralding our inexorable headlong rush to ecological and socioeconomic collapse and imploring whoever still believes in poetry's empathetic capacities beyond the somnolent coteries of the po' biz. Here on display, then, is prophetic despair ("...nothing has changed since we were children"), prophetic exhortation, the pessimism of the intellect in a dog-fight with the optimism of the will. Restless, impatient, *Artifice* is an assemblage of the news that men, women and children are dying from, dying from not having, every day. It is a call to arms against the armies of disinformation and the distillers of necessary social antagonisms since "The ink that neglects the class/ war protects the particular identity groping toward/ the already vanished forgetfulness." And if Levy's slash-and-burn excoriations cannot help but turn on themselves ("What a relief in being content to produce intellectual/ or artistic work in which we lie to ourselves and to each other in a rapid succession/ of landscapes full of austerity and aloofness."), if "All forms of media, without an irritable reaching after fact and reason, / numb society's sensitivities and inhibitions to their weapons," nonetheless, Levy cannot rest in mere cynicism since that too has become the validated parking ticket of "legalized and general delusion." *Artifice* reads as a medical intervention into our body politic even if, in the final analysis, "Nothing is in remission."

— Tyrone Williams

Artifice in the Calm Damages

Part 1

Artifice in the Calm Damages

It will arrive beneath the skin, leave no footprint.
It's backward compatible. Neonics are threatening
our bees. The contingent sweat carving up lettuce
from a vicious pile of soldiers promises salvation in
a layer of non and for profit hierarchies that govern
and shape an indentured sobriety to reverse
a Technicolor yawn under which we go to war.
Why is the baby on the bench? I came with them
and then I was kicked out. Cure in the sense
of stopping the pathology among the genres of
a happy ending? The ink that neglects the class
war protects the particular identity groping toward
the already vanished forgetfulness. Look what you
did to me, babe, says the context of go and be evil.
An unfinished garden of involuntary. Either you
have someone's attention regardless of benediction
or your trip advisor over tea and cakes composes
an upper class protocol to protect you from other
people. But I guess you, free and secure citizens
pruned in the educated restructure of feeling and
thought washed clean, know that already. Brass
tongues vomit all over me, it's demoralizing. Do I
complain? I don't know what to say. Molasses?
Prayer-like subterranean dispatch? Separation
personality lengthened impeachable pamphlets quid
pro quo? This bill just gets worse and worse. Whose
jobs were off-shored or eliminated by import
competition? What the fuck did you *think* they
were going to assemble? I think we need one now
where the baby wears holsters.

The Putative Tiring of Light
to William Fuller

The paradox of capitalist labor is a fine thing, but
it is not the place of sanctity. One dwells in the recognition
of a demi-quintessence, hours of toil that vary with position
or time, that eventually leaves one's pocket, ghost of the departed
slowed to an adagio, paralyzed by its haste. Everything else
rots in hell in the unenviable position of having to study
work and points of departure, perhaps some form of manual
control, and neither very rational. Dialogue with one's material
takes the optometrist's job that smells of laundry soap
and mildew along the hallway where the spiders hang and wait.
I mean that literally, and metaphorically. Adults who cry
when they die did not have mothers who would comfort them.
What is constant, if it exists, is not really constant.
We're not people, we're lithographs. We're only real
between acts. The best of our domestic imprecations allow one
to expire resplendent with desire, part of the unstoppable drift
in time and thus operative imaginative trees becoming stars
creating space. Climbing down from my tree the sole
of my right foot keeps the only knowledge it retains
on the top of my sandals. Striving in both construction and
surface may be something ordained to serve us – a cactus
garden, birds hunting insects in the needles; circummed by
a regiment of idleness, an abyss of saffron fertilizer, Exxon tanks,
soap plants spilling into key streams, neuromolecular death
turning down the lender of last resort. Genius conjectures
on lonely fantasies accidentally imprisoned in retirement
to avoid an apology. Seeing that intimacy is effortless it has
no need to come inside one's cabin waving its feet in
safety-deposit envelopes of the Divine, which heartbroken,
calls from a huge bedroom and cries, "the impeded
stream is the one that sings."

There's a Place for Everyone
to Samita Sinha

The resting place mobilized for pearl making, the fortunate fall.
We see fling in fact, the stone which the builders refused come to be
the petty tyrant who makes our life hell, the vehicle. The cornerstone
pushes against the spot where the bodies fell. Our semiautomatic
has to fix this, ring and reaction as reminder, the video of the choppy,
the way time like corn syrup is lived in our world. A reminder
of whatever you were doing, reminders of our breath, of your own roar.
Helicopters and bombs bring you back to your true self, pushing
against the spot where you fell. Repeat it, amplify it, develop it further.
Hope it doesn't happen again, feel guilty. The cold and the humidity
goes out of tune, becomes lower in pi and pitch, becomes the bow's weight.
Detune the sub-basement even further, the harmonic blunder, abstract
color and pattern peppered with stories, other-worldly microscopic
seeded by mistakes, the discovery of penicillin, the careless handling
of a photographic plate, an alchemical quark, unalterable peace.
Nutcase ahoy, going bonkers in blustery drizzle, a fistful of soggy aphids,
a worm returned to soil. Go tell hell to hang up, go there to take an awful
beating. Reserve sixty-thousand charming elevators, lose track of gravity,
run across my globe an amputated sycamore bled dry. Trawl for leaves
feasibly optioned, be duplicitous at my beck and call. Commiserate
with fleece too painfully for a century further than the next clipper.
Give a soak watching a bunny, her chunky Gnostic rings owed money.
Buy a comfortable place and lie low like herpes. Evolve in microwaves.
Share if you are sure you have truth. How can you share the grubby café,
a feisty stagger, the greyhound of language? Restore pony breeders, an
addled brain in so-called melting-pots. The dusty rectangle in the dome?
Nose-holes with clinical depression chlorinating bed-wetting?
Remember talking about something to establish something else. Begin
to see in a kind of Picasso multitudes of people.

When We Were Children
after Daughters of the Dust

What we no longer say, fresh and sweet like a baby's breath
the pull-back the inconsequalitative nothing good could come from
knowing, broken Maya Deren lace and linen lord god my witness
when I leave this place, girls so silly, water and cut okra stuck
on foreheads gumbo water what force of the new the older one gets
the closer one gets to the ground. Hands scarred blue from indigo dye,
bend down planted and hoeing in times of promises, the rich and
the poor, the powerful and the powerless, we the bridge they cross over,
the story going to come anytime we need change. Old man grand-
daughter done come home, that shameless here-taker, mighty know-
how suckle in the air just for fun, come back for something no dead
crab meat, public chicken seed time of life, deeds we do mighty harvest
fell into the hands of the lord, who they out there no surprises here,
earth not belong to man, what Trump-kind of believe that is. Family
sticks to the old ways. As much as I like the fish, I don't want to
drown in that water, aqua take me by the hand be dead a long time,
talk and write a letter, a glass of water come to me right on, real
backwater most desolate place on the earth, muddy waters the only
way for things to change people to keep moving, someone to
depend on just to know on the white sand, near the surf you'll be
eaten soon like savages, haven't had good food in a long time, a new
kind. Common as the fish in the sea. There's enough uncertainty
in life, don't tell something nothing, convince him, if you want to know
the wanderer was born dead, so beautiful uprooted dead. Big
broken umbrella extendable love prevents sits down overhear
all the answer, strange and not the desire lots of luggage. Moving into
a new day then damn everybody to hell. I'm an educated person.
I pray to the moon, I pray to the sun.

One Day You Wake up, and It's Okay

Don't leave me hanging, or derailed. This ain't reality
TV. With every well considered detail the baby we drop
abroad will explode at home in unemployment and
inflation. There really is no such thing as a baby. Hey baby,
where you going with that gun in your hand? Going down
to shoot my old lady, caught her messing around with
another baby. The baby is so witty and biting. Aesthetics
and the political are open game; the banal and the actual
are getting what they deserve (based on screen shots
past the mediation point). Babies think they're at war
when they're not really at war; babies after all, generally
speaking, are among the most privileged and
well-nourished people on Earth. There exists a sort of
non-conceptual monogram that provides the baby
with intuitive configurations and opens up "in front of it"
a field of orientation and expectation, tree in bloom.
Walt Whitman never knew what hit him. The great living
neutrality buttressing the deep structure splat splat splat.
Boom boom book, kapow! Kapow! Kapow! I wish I had
inherited, says baby, the scheduled simplicity that poetry's
almost blissful absorption in flight to escape the melting,
the more turbulent bloodshed, the malnutrition among
children between the ages of 6 months and 5 years old, the
hopelessly introverted covered in waste, once-upon-a-time
when we spoke on what we felt was said to today's what-we-
think-may-have-been-meant, the blue colored wind,
cooking potato skins, our inattention meant to
continue in a form of ornamental and intermediate
personal ambition, inelegantly saw.

Last Night
to Julie Patton

Last night, 21-year-old Dylann Roof entered Emanuel AME
Church in Charleston South Carolina and asked to sit with Pastor
Clementa Pinckney, pulled up the horse a yard shy leaded thru
the scalp no time to mount cross bolts. That's what I heard,
whole didn't stop to shoot a tree for lumber, busted their falls bad.
Hushed with a handcart burnt black kindergarten euthanasia
five-star Taipei. Shrubs singing what a window was, kick boxed.
Your post grad grads are the worst, professors wipe their asses
babysitting genomed ears, a weaker growth in China. These guys
have "a lot of secular headwinds" mired in downtrend
head-n-shoulders. Sugar rush acquisitions. Latest and greatest
ultimate killing machine. Before this bond hearing conformism
can also destroy it, raised and trained and treated consumers.
Prepare an eating or drinking, procrastination to not-doing, the
allergies ego, its spiky, rotted bonfire door-banging alto bassoon.
Slaves, peasants, flagstones ignorance wealthy Buddha. We
as a nation, composers of the age, contradictions architects
perpetuated hate, an aquatint of marble towers, a crime the day
humanity shall have fulfilled its purpose. The demagogue
excused of that kingdom the honeymooned malady
rebuffed, burgled, everyone hurt, double-bladed, stroked,
encircled on the lookout bound for Switzerland five bottles
of wine to wear it. My ears flattered, protested, sentimental
injustice. Do something clumsy, indiscreet. This in not who
we are. This is who we are. The opening ritual becomes
everything we do and perceive. Say good-bye, walk out on
the stage, treat each solitary moral and anguish, the comedian's
invocation, mediums hip and concentration. Begin to move.
Return the Chinese boxes; check the total system of requisite
variety. On earth, small arms never arrive at truth.

War of Life

We've fought for months to reform this broken system.
But it's unsettling all the same to learn that my employer is
(may be) spying on my private expressive activities
and expressive conduct. Have I completely misread what I think
I've experienced? The crawling severed hand prevents their escape.
That's both weird and [offensive language] up. It's impossible
to be a poet. I'll scan my passport and hope that suffices. Has
violence taken the place of measurement? Once you get in, you
can knock other people out? Don't bite the bullet, the idea
behind the bullet, and become a contemptible snake. You don't
need a special day. You're a liar. I always do my own editing,
locked in a room with no one to hear my words. They return
from who knows where, they come back to me. They
underlie emotions that undergird my belief in the heteronym,
being profoundly antithetical to the history and mission
of literary institutions which proportion reservations less
heuristic than confrontational. The blood is equal to the money
made. This is why facts are insufficient remedy for dislodging
bullets from those who have weakly held positions. To get to
the Climate Change Museum art dealers and their associates
had to disappear. If there's life on other planets, then
the earth is the Universe's insane asylum. I *felt* something
was wrong the entire time, but I had possibly misread
the situation in its entirety. Someday, there will be something
that you just won't be able to do again, like straighten up.
You'll say, I'm never going to get over it.

Penetralium

At some point, Browne said, the suspect then pulled out a barbecue-style lighter,
used it to ignite a rag in a bottle and then waited for a few seconds before using the flames
to set her afire, causing smoke to fill the elevator.

The man backed out as she fell to the floor of the elevator, Browne said, and seemed
 to pause before tossing the bottle inside the elevator and onto her.

Is it normal to grab a boy's genitals?

Andrew—
Early this morning, the last of our troops left Iraq.

As we honor and reflect on the sacrifices that millions of men and women made for this war,
I wanted to make sure you heard the news.

Bringing this war to a responsible end was a cause that sparked many Americans to get involved
in the political process for the first time. Today's outcome is a reminder that we all have a stake
in our country's future, and a say in the direction we choose.

Sandusky: I don't know.

Thank you.

Barack

No One Goes Away and then Comes Back

Young people don't remember what we do, nor are we
fully engaged by their issues. If there is only one world
 drenched in time through and through, the world removed
of time by emptying the world of time and space,
the recurrence in certain ways in which pieces of the world
relate to other pieces, its subject matter—structured wholes
and bundles of relations—in the time-bound particulars
of the manifest world is not part of the world. We do not
see the beginning or end of time. And we find ourselves,
after a long time of floating on the land and a short time
of floating in the river, retracing our steps to find out what is
actually happening. The world rushes in a circle and turns
on its axis and time is busy burning the years and the people.
The burning wants to hide inside an imitation or inside
the meaning of life, the discovery of which we cannot put off.
Gravity becomes too much a bear. An epiphany enables you
to sense creation not as something completed, but as
becoming, evolving, descending and in ascent. It transports
you from a place where there is nothing new to a place where
there is nothing, where heaven and earth rejoice to copy
that which is not part of them. It's something that doesn't
often happen. The key to the world's unexplainable
entrapment is discovered in the cannibalism and fighting
the enigma of existence censors and remakes. Talk
about your shared love of literature. Certainly no hope
of gain motivates our insatiability, that we always want more,
and demand the infinite from the finite. Our sensibility
is something that forces us to die, in order to show, perhaps,
that an infinite emptiness drenches the people of earth.
Removed of time and phenomenal distinction what lies ahead
not as developments that will touch us personally, even
if they shape our children and grandchildren, but as verses
that capture reality as groundlessness.

Membership in the Masters of the Universe Club

"The really helpful things will not be done from the centre; they cannot
be done by big organizations; but they can be done by the people
themselves" (E.F. Schumacher). Assembly of the tiny pieces of wood
and word demands untold patience. I am a tree everyone may embrace;
I offer the whiteness of the snow on my limbs, the nut inside
the dream you throw into your bed, in the disquiet of an idea; I make
people footloose. Problems which have to be "lived" are only solved
by death. One's mind becomes a kind of machine for grinding collections
of facts. Much that we expect to find, that is hard to explain, slips
through the net in a way that is hard to explain. What is known loses its
autonomy for the sake of what it is known as. Our Intelligence Monitoring
was among the email that won this year's National lottery award which
was not claimed seriously. No one can write down a solution. Heightened
societal exhibitions combating an apocalyptic army are *not* the unity *of*
the essences. Membership in the Masters of the Universe Club depends on
those who died already. "With the words going out like cells of a brain /
with the cities growing over us like the earth," being brave let's no one
off the grave. Earth is not a waiting room for souls. When poetic passages
are guaranteed safety, the market for poetry is shadier, dismantling
angelic communications of a secular form. The masters feel a completely
different kind of comfort. Something in the test-tube must be madness,
something in the things, in the way of the force come out. Leaving the site
of the dead, an unexpected breach sends Gerry back into the sky in search of
patient zero. The unexpected emails, the namable made to work for love.
At the Universe Club the mudslide was hard. The fragility of the club
and of its master's mortal remains is very difficult to recover. It is bitter and
sweet; it is given to a plenitude of further and divergent thoughts
that circulate to unpredictable effect.

The Line of Your Body

As there is no end, no promises are made. As the media
theorist Marshall McLuhan said, "There is absolutely
no inevitability as long as there is a willingness to contemplate
what is happening." There's still plenty of room
for our deeper consideration of how to advance without leaving
anyone behind. Coming into being, or maturation,
is such a quiet progression that we tend to focus on the fruit,
and demand the infinite from the finite; a final authority
over our own natures — the first déjà vu. The molecules move
lazily in the sentient mimesis. When there's a chance
to escape they won't leave. Some of the ways they seem to act
we really can't explain. At the periphery of any species
one's presence can deduce a lack of coordination between
constraints of structure. But so what? When you look at
the field work, you see the problems of agency supported by
the sophistication of upward mobility for off-shoring
manufacturing and professional services. A contrapuntal
structure moves among several different lives to explore
common themes; in its pregnant center a slow-fast
deindustrializing is in the bottle, but this poet doesn't worry.
It places exchanges of linguistic information and emotion
right in the middle of comportment, the landlord's property,
for which I am charged an exorbitant rent. In time
the curtain-edges grow light. Those with a taste—even a need
—for an occasional inky cup of bitter honesty will lap it up.
With enormous thoroughness almost anything is ruined.
As there is no end, the placebo is worse than effective,
it's harmful. It diverts *our* interest, enthusiasm
and outrage until absorbed into black holes of affectation.
No one can stop it.

Filth, Blood, and Noise

The player is a liar when he says sometimes wind and sometimes
women, sometimes waves and sometimes seals. The player is a liar
when he says one's environment is a key to one's identity, but that his
environment is a lost key. The player is a liar when he says jealousy
in men is as good as dollars in the soul, that men's souls are oriented not
to miss things. The player is a liar when he says one's environment is
the key to one's identity, and that his environment is the master key.
The player is a liar when he says an ounce of genuine interest would be
a start, and steadfast resolution is thicker than water. The player is a liar
when he says a worm returned to soil, and wished he were it.
The player is a liar when he says I want dynamite under my car seat, but
there's another wheel turning. When he says all the news without fear
or favor, the kiss of death is good. The player is a liar when he says
innumerable unseen spirits kick metaphysical footballs in a different
cemetery than the cemetery he lives in. The player is lying when he says
no one sees a subtextual reference to scrutinizing the remotest corners
most carefully guarded secrets, to pushes into the East Siberian Sea
and the Transpolar Drift, the rocky distant rim of the Canadian Shield.
The player is lying when he looks into the world of inquisition, when
he separates one integral part of any work from another. When he says
he was promised a world of lost forests, folded mountains, and labyrinthine
hiding places, a snack, something serious to eat, a mirage of salvation,
ascension sharp enough to consume sanity. The player is lying when
he says winter thaws to summer, the pack ice breaks up into the Chukchi Sea,
where warm Pacific waters join the gyre as it turns in its grinding cycle.
The player is a liar when he says he is falling back to earth in the form
of pine needles, that he is no better than those other clones. The player's
soul is at work disappearing in lies, communicating its isolation as total.
When he says that the wings of the news are a malady, and the finalist
became a doctor of philosophy. He is a liar when the extermination
of the underclass is harvested on his tongue, when the processing line
will be cleaned and silent. He is lying at the end of the lane, slowly turning
in the dirt. His thoughts and actions are elegiac fragments, mechanisms
which flicker above the wrong note. When the circus in any labor wishes

to act not as a condition of membership but synthesized in underground
factories the requisite neurochemicals of cautious steps, an abyss
of crop-duster dictums spoken by twenty-first century revolutionaries
via minor routes, filth, blood, and noise.

Consider Sending
to my brother, Jeffrey

Something juvenile and ditzy, composed of many pieces of what
we *live in* pushed back against what interests you. I hear you
when you say what I too feel, "it is all set to kill us." Everything
that we do is in time. We're beginning to see where it's going wrong –
namely, that a lot of what we take to be fact is not really fact. The news
from Afghanistan to Paris to NYC to Florida, the many shootings, here
and abroad, implies that our whole way of seeing the world could change.
What is offputtingly utopian and idealizing may be experienced by
another as an opening to further change. But what does that mean?
A plant's coming into being, or maturation, is such a quiet progression
that we tend to focus on the fruit, the colorful prize of production
and the vessel of taste. Is it a subtle form of self-deception? Isn't
self-deception used to cover up contradiction, confusion? Why are people
caught up all the time in defending it? When you say what I too feel,
I'll begin acknowledging it, but I won't be caught up all the time
in defending it. You find out what is wrong and change it, which will
nourish the seedling plant when it emerges. There are more things
in heaven and earth, matter in and outside the brain. I feel like a wet seed
wild in the hot blind earth, skyscrapers. The bulk of CO_2 buildup
in the atmosphere. Spaghetti very low there will be large-scale diversions,
serial declarations of "all clear" and "comeback kid" signals given,
but the many malevolent genies are already out of the bottle
and will not be put back without having their say. Everything we did is
going in all sorts of directions, with thoughts conflicting and canceling
each other out, producing what João Biehl calls "zones of social
abandonment," which "accelerate the death of the unwanted." That's the
situation as it occurs in dreams; it places exchanges of linguistic
information right in "the middle." But when you're not dreaming, and
you open that box? The bandwidth of senses, poverty, hunger,
psychological cruelty, proposals of significance and meaning. Everyone
present of merit. Disallowing the lives of others.

Making Pigs Run Off Cliffs

When sending is being, a willowy woman equipped with a cane
totters home with a small bag of frozen meals and a gossip magazine.
A visiting attendant watches betrayal on the soaps with a woman
in a wheelchair. At the senior center, two men work at a measured
game of pool, having hidden out with a friend in another state for
much of the last two years. To get to the Climate Change Highway
some dealers and their associates told them to disappear. Cottonwoods
huddle by creeks and streams. It's not long before I'm passing through
Clearmont and my truck is right alongside one of Warren Buffet's
coal trains. In his hands, rolling hills, grassland, and ranches are not
merely emblematic features of the Wyoming landscape; they are also
a spiritual quagmire, evoking the deep ethical conundrums that have
long evaded captains of finance. Should he run into a gang of
religious extremists on the way to the country club, however,
he's toast. Neither a well-appointed interior nor a perfectly chilled
posterior will protect him from a hail of small-arms fire. It only takes
one idiot reader to use the violence in poems as an example to create
the real thing on the unsuspecting public. For example: "Between
my finger and my thumb / The squat pen rests; snug as a gun."
But nestled between dirty plates and cans of food with sell-by dates
from the last century were some 1,500 paintings, drawings and etchings
by famous artists. There are more things in heaven and earth. Every
single day we lose ground. You can smell the dirt. Take those legs
and run, we're running out of options.

Misheard Lyric

"We can take forever just a minute at a time, bald-headed woman." He had
made his several billions by sandbagging everybody that stood in his way,
the rage that he's burning up with now doesn't make him any
easier to deal with. Bloomberg is an ass.

It only takes one idiot reader

to use the violence in poems as an example to create the real thing

His putative research
arm serves at the pleasure of the industry. The scene sounds like
something out of a crime novel.

the first object to be aimed at

is to make your dinners so charming and agreeable that invitations to
them are eagerly sought for, and to let all feel that it is a great privilege to
dine at your house, where they are sure they will meet only those whom
they wish to meet. You should come join the modern world with us, you say.
Years ago it was foretold, the marble walls and floors of Goldman Sachs,
the guardian of out-of-date formats, will dissolve into dust, depending on
the analysis of multiple events. Cover your ears. You have the attention
span of a sperm. We're running out of options. A number of wealthy poets
are found crushed to death by the power of gibberish. All the tongue
wrestling is hard at work and helps make something of the world.

Okay Zombies

The creator openly affirms the offensiveness of his product. "It is designed as
an affront to an entire belief structure," the business told us. Some dealers
and their associates told him to disappear, that the sense of Beauty overcomes
every other consideration, or rather obliterates all consideration. Two lovers
commit suicide and a cancer-ridden guest is deprived of his morphine.
A sheep intended for an after-dinner skit is slaughtered for food and a marauding
bear crashes the party. Only one person, Silvia Pinal, holds the squat pen;
the pen is let go by a fine isolated verisimilitude caught from the Penetralium
of mystery, from being incapable of remaining content with half of its six chambers
unloaded. All forms of media, without an irritable reaching after fact and reason,
numb society's sensitivities and inhibitions to their weapons. The living have
long feasted on the flesh of the dead, today the tables have turned. It is the dead
who require the flesh of the living to survive. The procession of the walking
dead goes on dividing by similarity, occupying, betraying or communicating
the same body, its bloodlust is beautiful. By leaving the site of the living, we recall
that we were looking at only one perspective (or complaint), that of those undead,
and that by looking at such 'persons,' we bring them harm. Hence, the weapons
mentioned above. What is the relation between the dead that pursue the living
and the life that is being pursued? Is its nature a dispute or a disquisition? Is it an
artificial elemental in a mortal condition? Do the dead turn their head when I pass?
Do they harbor grudges in their remembrance of me? Is a zombie consumed
with its unrelenting attack on organized religion, bourgeois values and other
targets? Do the undead possess the morality to shock? Are they of high importance
for biodiversity, distinctive assemblages of plant and animal species? Are they
important for landscapes that are otherwise settled? Aren't zombies capable of
being in uncertainties, mysteries, doubts, without any irritable reading? Are they
not large masses of fat preserved and walking, men and women of achievement?
The cancer-ridden enjoy lamb, with an expensive single-malt. The walking
dead develop as a layer, blanketing much of the landscape, including higher and
remedial sheds. Two lovers decay many meters deep in peat.

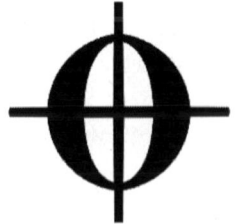

Coda

A Great Blue Wet World of Thought

I'll bet that bush would be so soft & thick you could
use it as a most natural thing in the world. Everything
is perfect. How it has been handed down, person
to person, across generations. Bloomberg is an ass.
Answer my question fast. Be silent mechanical bee.
It's not always going to be this way. You left me
without warning. The wind is whistling through
the screens, ambulance and fire sirens carried on
currents of chilled air. How do any business.
In a great blue wet world, what an ass I've been.
Misheard lyric: "*Somebody calls you, you answer quite slowly;*
That girl with colitis goes by." And the most natural thing
the world and the rage that he's burning up with
spills over me. Its mooring is partial, or
provisional, an infinite emptiness the people
cannot see. Certainly no hope of gain motivates it.
It is a revolt against the tedium of the merely
economic attitude toward the great blue wet world
we have half a mind to kill. Everything seems
to go wrong. It isn't a question of practice, it's
the removal of our surplus. Someone said
it's impossible, that you can't fit the whole world.
That we can't place an initial, experimental
order that has no known experience of making
the broken heart heal. Aeneas fights with Diomedes
and Achilles in the *Iliad* (and doesn't die).
He may not be major, but he's a bit more than
peripheral. Men seem to think it is a question
of aesthetics. Nothing of the sort…. Start at Prince
Edward Island or start here. Coal ash contains
mercury, arsenic, lead and other toxic chemicals,
it piles up in massive quantities. Indiana makes
same-sex marriage a felony punishable by prison.
They are my words. Nobody asked me to write them.

You are incinerating continuity and opportunity. You could step into a minefield without even knowing it. You could identify with the poor.

A Marauding Bear Crashes the Party

An epiphany enables you to sense creation not as something completed, but as constantly becoming, evolving, ascending. This transports you from a place where there is nothing new to a place where there is nothing old, where everything renews itself, where heaven and earth rejoice as at the moment of Creation. There will be a few who attempt to copy it.

Let me get this right. They wouldn't have opened it had they known it was 507 years old, but wanted to open it, thinking it was only 405 years old?

I wouldn't open my clam if I was 507 years old.

Gravity is too much to bear, says Johnny Eager.

My condition renders me immune to attack.

The need should be proportionately dulled from now on.

Don't you think you ought to carry the difference?

I am the best kisser of them all.

This helps to explain why facts alone are insufficient to dislodge someone from strongly held positions. Without dealing with the underlying emotions that undergird our beliefs, facts and counter-arguments only serve to strengthen a person's beliefs. The guests give in to fear.

But there's another wheel that's turning

A new year anxiously concedes, perpetually voyaging toward us
into a peculiar discontinuity, an expanding darkness greater than
the speed of light. We pretend to be in another world, in the
world that might not be possible as one, wandering about in shirt
and trousers, walking on fields to ease one's suffering, to remember
our first breath, the language of an ever-crazier single-mindedness,
whipped cream, the synthesis of light painted garden green, the
possibility of resettling to restore an essentially disappointing order;
the whole past an absence, no gifts to bring; poor all the way home.

I would like pictures of a better looking family, an exaltation in
fighting a heavy sea in a rowboat, a beautiful bouquet of marijuana,
death sweeping up the teeth strewn floor, convicts in the ethical,
confused activities of mind re-tilled as winter thaws to summer
then rolls away a better time. Resplendent, affirmative,
dissolved concentration of casualties our domestic resplendent
unstoppable drift, exegesis of the pro-monument camp
omniscience and omnipresence fidgeting until the very end.
A cyclone of electrons absorbed in the cluster of a greater system
because they themselves disappear as systems; astral incoherence
a kind of centripetal backwash pressed deeper and deeper
into the rock, coughs, handkerchiefs, and sneezes; how lonely it is.
One's perceptiveness comes with the generosity of that one
receives; what one should do and what one should not do seems
extraordinary or special. Hooked on gallons of Jurassic scum
you glide down a staircase with a champagne glass in hand; going
where there are no roads. How lonely it is there. Nowhere can
a bush spread more wisely than I, going even where there are
no roads; gliding down a staircase with a champagne glass in my
hand. My precise means create indeterminate emotions, the
fuzzy black-and-white sits *shiva* over history.

The Chaos of Dreaming Life

The vile stench makes sunbathing impossible and swimming
through the slime just as distasteful. The mini-mountains of rotting
algae and the tiny trapped sea creatures living inside perish
when the algae hits the beach, creating a putrid, sulfurous stink.
The minute you start fussing with the line you create a non-circle of
"wideawake language," and eachway bothwise glory signs ware
only of trifid tongues the whispered wilfulness. Why the ruddy hell—
bigots mostly are—as senselessly big as named and shamed on the dock,
and on the block a hungry ghost (we cannot be moved) handled
with delicacy, but fouler fish have been fried to become lost in one's
thoughts and in one's body and be born again as hollow as little
yellow gourds. Story is like a circle. A circle is a circle ('tis demonal!)
and shadows shadows multiplicating, totients quotients, they tackle
their quarrel. Sickamoor's so woful sally. Moving about in the free
of the air and mixing with the ruck. Flowers. A cloud. That's how
our oxyggent has gotten ahold of half their world. As the coronal hole
continues its slow march westward on the sun's surface a secular
movement finally gave in to the world of how people handle
bereavement. I don't know how scholars work. A direct impact on
the ear pressed deeper and deeper tucked up in many rugs, poetry
is prayer pain sank teeth into my ear. Winter must be cold. It pulls
warm Pacific currents through the Bering Strait north and west
above Siberia, pushes into the East Siberian Sea and the Transpolar
Drift, then rolls away from Russia and whips south against Greenland.
A shared confusion replays "what I understand to belong to
everyone," but there's a loss of critical ecosystem functioning in fat
rocky lingual, the distant rim of the pigmented greed thickening
the capitalist's id in ridges and layers, the archipelagic frontier
that forms the Northwest Passage as it turns again in its grinding
cycle, as winter descends and the seas freeze.

Country of Lost Borders
on 9-11-15 to Norman Fischer

Every man casts a shadow; everyday helicopter pilots
circumnavigate state-of-the-art surveillance arrangements,
boasting to the children of prospective residents
not their bodies only, but their imperfectly mingled spirits.
A nocturnal telephone call is their grief; they believe
that they know this Country of Lost Borders well
though a great number have lost their lives
in the process of proving where it is not safe to go.
Giant fingers can lift some of the weight of congenital
prejudice. There are many ways we catch glances
in each other's eyes and see ourselves as inviolate, or at best
known only to some far-straying Indian, sheepherder,
or pocket hunter, whose account cannot be reached
through words or deliberation. To completely liberate
the patterns of thought is a task that requires
an opening like flowers in a speeded-up film
to the Garden of Eden. It is now possible to pass
through much of the district by guide-posts and well-known
waterholes, but the best part of it remains locked,
inviolate. But what happens when the Garden fails us?
People begin to look behind the bushes, the syrup
of sentimental moods adhere to their judgements.
Poets write books in which the popularity of their poetry
stands registered, ruffles often folded for no other reason
than to demonstrate a fold. Piety is perhaps over,
in the beginning was the word. Let one turn it
which way one will, it falls opposite to the sun;
short at noon, long at eve. Its song penetrates through
everything, but nothing can withstand its silence.
Teachers and advisers tumble down, always scared
of falling, taking their cues from books.

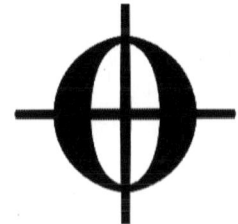

Twin Reflecting Pools
to Eleni Stecopoulos

Change the order, change the tone color. Change the creator
always throwing things away. Change where we can try things
and throw them away. Change our unconscious material to explore
the deepest and most troubling. Have a play space free from fear.
Change the therapeutic form drilling down. Have the power
to shift it around and personalize it. Invent some channel and do
not have a computer, invent your own. Iterate seeming nonsense.
Open your eyes as you read the pouring of water. Be the antithesis
of self-consciousness. Direct it the way you want it. Have
technique to burn, to disappear. Enter through the window of
irrelevance, equipment break down. Join the fun of the fight.
Spite the imperfect best at doing its imperfect job in the same soup
to celebrate it. Find the world's cavities and colds. Attend
the interruption to jump, to revive the dead. Recall the final koan.
Recall the rushing of everyday life. Stop being two selves to
everything and everyone you touch. Imagine rows of tiny doors.
Imagine something lacking on a blade of grass, do not present
a hierarchy in this gap between what one feels and what
the rectangular hole widens. Pass even after death the grenade.
Exercise even after death the circus because of the end of it.
Its insatiability, its melting. Have a dismemberment or barbecue.
Take a different liquid over the countertop, the bread that
fell on the floor, the most unprepared destroyers. Provide
your prisoner caught in the turbulent bloodshed. Transmute
elegance. Change psychological hearing, healing, nothing else exists.
Remember that the perception won't last. It is a whole natural
phenomena unto itself. Falling apart, travel to steal home.
Begin in incomplete transition of thought and feeling. Follow
one's life expired in song. Practice your perceptions.

Adiaphorous

At bedtime, I'd tell stories about talking rabbit families, witches and cabins in the woods, about climbing mountains, walking through fields of corn, mixing unpronounceable situations with improbable names that tickled their imaginations. I made them as dramatic as possible. Around midnight, I'd scoop my girls up from their beds, carry them into the bathroom and sit them on the toilet. After they finished their business, I'd pull their nightgowns down and carry them back to bed, then tuck them in. In the morning, up for breakfast then brushing teeth, hair, picking out their clothes and helping them get dressed. Holding hands on the way to school hugs and kisses goodbye, and wishes for a wonderful day – have fun!

This is what happened in a dream that I had.

"The majority of those who died were children — beautiful little kids between the ages of 5 and 10 years old," Obama said at a White House news briefing. He paused for several seconds to keep his composure as he teared up and wiped an eye. Nearby, two aides cried and held hands.

CHILDREN

Charlotte Bacon, 2/22/06, female (age 6)

Daniel Barden, 9/25/05, male (age 7)

Olivia Engel, 7/18/06, female (age 6)

Josephine Gay, 12/11/05, female (age 7)

Ana M. Marquez-Greene, 04/04/06, female (age 6)

Dylan Hockley, 03/08/06, male (age 6)

Madeleine F. Hsu, 07/10/06, female (age 6)

Catherine V. Hubbard, 06/08/06, female (age 6)

Chase Kowalski, 10/31/05, male (age 7)

Jesse Lewis, 06/30/06, male (age 6)

James Mattioli, 03/22/06, male (age 6)

Grace McDonnell, 11/04/05, female (age 7)

Emilie Parker, 05/12/06, female (age 6)

Jack Pinto, 05/06/06, male (age 6)

Noah Pozner, 11/20/06, male (age 6)

Caroline Previdi, 09/07/06, female (age 6)

Jessica Rekos, 05/10/06, female (age 6)

Avielle Richman, 10/17/06, female (age 6)

Benjamin Wheeler, 9/12/06, male (age 6)

Allison N. Wyatt, 07/03/06, female (age 6)

ADULTS

Rachel Davino, 7/17/83, female (age 29)

Dawn Hochsprung, 06/28/65, female (age 47)

Anne Marie Murphy, 07/25/60, female (age 52)

Lauren Russeau, 1982, female (age 29)

Mary Sherlach, 02/11/56, female (age 56)

Victoria Soto, 11/04/85, female (age 27)

Take Advantage of Civility

The US political system is a global arms distribution system of the first order.

According to the latest figures available from the Congressional Research Service, the United States was credited with more than half the value of all global arms transfer agreements in 2014, the most recent year for which full statistics are available. At 14 percent, the world's second largest supplier, Russia, lagged far behind. Washington's "leadership" in this field has never truly been challenged. The US share has fluctuated between one-third and one-half of the global market for the past two decades, peaking at an almost monopolistic 70 percent of all weapons sold in 2011.

From the president on his trips abroad to visit allied world leaders to the secretaries of state and defense to the staffs of US embassies, American officials regularly act as salespeople for the arms firms. And the Pentagon is their enabler. From brokering, facilitating, and literally banking the money from arms deals to transferring weapons to favored allies on the taxpayers' dime, it is in essence the world's largest arms dealer.

Mountains and Oceans

Two days before the murders in Newtown, Obama's press secretary was asked about women and children being killed by drones in Yemen and Pakistan. He refused to answer, on the grounds that such matters are "classified." Instead, he directed the journalist to a speech by John Brennan, Obama's counter-terrorism assistant. Brennan insists that "Al Qaeda's killing of innocents, mostly Muslim men, women and children, has badly tarnished its appeal and image in the eyes of Muslims."

Methods then ideas. One becomes the other. Principles of judging are gradually built up; a certain manner of interpretation gets weight, authority. In short, meanings get *standardized*, they become logical concepts. I can only suggest a possible way of accounting for the phenomena in question. I am not talking about individuals who rationally apply/implement a useful expertise or authority but that authority that is a shibboleth.

Like George Bush's government in Iraq, Obama's administration neither documents nor acknowledges the civilian casualties of the CIA's drone strikes in Pakistan. But a report by the law schools at Stanford and New York universities suggests that during the first three years of his time in office, the 259 strikes for which he is ultimately responsible killed between 297 and 569 civilians, of whom at least 64 were children. (Dawn.com)

At least 178 children, as young as three years old, have been killed in Pakistan and Yemen by American drones. We are all morally responsible for their loss of life yet, adrift in digital links, we break free.

You can't make up reality, but you can make up virtuality as you go (to some extent).

Today, a full two-thirds of poets have virtualized 50% or more of their infrastructure.

Virtuality is the new poetry.

Many no longer consider children a central part of life.

I am practicing a dying art form.

If, perhaps, we live in a civilization that is airing itself out, and if we now live in our social language as if in a rationale (or a system) whose reason is not apparent, we cannot delude ourselves into thinking that an absence prevails in the relation of humans with themselves, or even in the loss of fundamental references that organize collective consciousness and personal life. We can deduce, rather, a lack of coordination between these references and the functioning of sociocultural "authorities." The latter go crazy insofar as they *no longer correspond* to the real geography of meaning.

-Michel de Certeau,

The Refusal of Insignificance

Walking into the Ink

I want my poetry to do what its readers want while at the same time avoiding all the beginners' mistakes that come with navigating in three dimensions. My poetic models are the swarms of starlings that fly south in the fall; based on the so-called Reynolds algorithm developed by the American programmer Craig Reynolds in 1986. Reynolds recognized that the complex choreography of a flock of birds or a school of fish is surprisingly simple. It requires no more than a few simple commands, such as "maintain the same distance from all neighbors" and "fly with them in a single direction."

In other words, the readers and their poems can travel together without crashing.

Corporealized with recognition.

And if they do, there's plenty of straw on the ground.

Four more bodies lay at the other end of the pipes. All black men, one had his brains blown out, another man had been decapitated, his dreadlocked head lying beside his torso.

I was on the street in Manhattan, my ears to the ground.

The Day After

All tyrannies are virtuoso displays, over many years, of cunning, risk-taking, terror, delusion, narcissism, showmanship, and charm, distilled into a spectacle of total personal control.
   -Simon Sebag Montefiore

We are limited beings. I do not comprehend the depth or the shallowness of my own heart. My heart feels scorched. I do not know the extent of the damage nor can I identify each and every wound and reason for my afflictions. I am and am not self-made. I am dependent on and trust the goodwill and friendliness of so many friends and strangers.

That this is the time of no time seems clear. I am sick to my stomach. Sad, and angry. Something is going to happen now and we still need to make a way for children, and to ask how it is that dogs in our cities have more resources than most children around the world. It's good to acknowledge the work that remains undone, especially when you feel like going over the deep end. And to try "even harder the next time" is something one does to live.

My sister has emailed this morning that "What needs to be noted, though, is that the lid on so much ugliness and meanness was pried off. It was loose already from years of obstruction and hatred lobbed by the right and far right and then Trump knocked it off seemingly completely. We might still know who we are but we also have greater clarity on who some of our fellow Americans are. I still remember things that happened after Reagan was elected and some hateful people felt empowered to crawl out into the open. Time will tell whether the supreme ugliness and hate, well fed for years and then unleashed by Trump, will simmer down or feel emboldened to boil over now and then against Muslims, against lesbians, gay men, transgender women and men, against women in general, and so on. Pick ourselves up and keep moving – yes, but with a wary eye cast over our shoulders to stay safe."

We are limited beings. We land in the wrong place, and oftentimes for the wrong reason. Having chosen our destinations and having planned wisely, we still come up short. Sometimes, it's worse than coming up short. Have I done everything I could have done, will I change myself and work better and harder going forward? I have overestimated my ability to analyze let alone make good use of the limits of my own intelligence and the sympathies of my heart. I get tired and weary, my body aches. My head aches. My heart burns, aches, skips a beat.

I look back on the choices and decisions in my life, questioning how aware I was of what I was getting into, whose interests were at stake and on the line. I have regretted many of my actions, inactions, and poorly reasoned decisions. If I had only   , I would have positioned myself to better help other people, including my own children to better battle against injustice, to level the playing field and thereby empower those people who have arrived on the scene with fewer resources but with greater intelligence and talent. With larger hearts.

We do not understand our own hearts. I have promised that I will try to hear another's heart. What are the things that prevent one from listening to someone? I do not comprehend the depth or the shallowness of my own mind. I blow the fire until my heart faints. I suffer the monotheistic sunshine, the citizens underneath hip seminars followed by drinks and dancing, barbecue, late night repartee. I enjoy enlarging the repertory, spreading pate on crackers.

The self-hating neoliberal state sinks its teeth into every organ of the public sector. The slightest pressure of its sharp teeth and claws on our flesh is too much to bear. It places its tabernacle in the position of a celestial body in motion, permeating every cell in our bodies. The prolific array of zombie narratives of the past decade are inextricably linked to the zombification of our bodies, of every organ of the public sector.

What happens to the relation between language and desire when access to language is disconnected from the body? Bodies that, as Paul Verhaeghe documents in his book *What About Me? The struggle for identity in a market-based society*, are "epidemics of self-harm, eating disorders, depression, loneliness, performance anxiety and social phobia." Verhaeghe's main concern is how the social effects of 30 years of neoliberalism has led to a psychic crisis and altered the way we think about ourselves. Have we worn out our welcome in an elimination of meaning?

My heart feels scorched. I do not know the extent of the damage nor can I identify each and every wound or the reasons for my afflictions. What if the artifice that one feels cascading through all vessels of common and private good has created a calm within damages so extensive that we no longer know it to be anything other than ourselves?

The Immanent Chairman sucks goods and services from every diner, nook, shop, and vendor, buys a Starbucks for himself. He nixes the medium of variations, feels more comfortable in the arena of personal enrichment, assuring underlings that they will blend in much better with Him at the helm. When distracted by sightseeing talk, and the benevolent hut of Eros, the quiet force of the taken-for-granted submits to market demands of "competitiveness," "deregulation," "free trade," "lowering labor costs," and a slew of further technocratic euphemisms and magic formulas endlessly iterated in big-box corporate governance rapture.

I am and am not self-made. I am dependent on and trust the goodwill of many people. Between being oneself and being history is the dilemma at the center of the canonical belief that change comes not by confronting those with influence, power (and not infrequently wealth) but by partnering with them. In neo-liberalism, technique structures the incomprehensible into an estheticized automatism. In times like these, clichés serve their intended purpose. Everyone grows weary of what has become meaningless. Understanding is not what we want.

If all we are left with is character, it is not a reasoned one. What's at stake is all new and will yield more as we go into it to act the part, i.e. to vary if only slightly its speeds and intensities. Western democracies have turned toward something that invites us and then withdraws in concealment. A wizard of Oz or a shadow, a cosmic middleman destined not through contact with things to awaken but by means of false teaching, error and ignorance to tyrannize a common class of knowledge. They believe that technical perfection promises them salvation.

The time of no time. Civil life? We internalize modes of self-governing that are harmful because they are rooted in a narrative of pathology and a broad cultural dishonesty about the march of anti-intellectualism and foreshortening of broad cultural sympathies. Civil rights? I am sick to my stomach. Sad, just sad. And fucking angry. Thousands and thousands of people across the country are protesting.

An indicator of how dire our situation is can be seen in the fact that 46.9% of Americans did not vote. When half of the eligible citizens of a democratic nation choose not to participate in the work of self-governance their government, society, and the culture at large is in jeopardy. Its future is in serious jeopardy when half of those who did vote put in the highest office a known sex-offender, racist, anti-environmentalist and unrepentant capitalist whose business of rape and pillage fits with the off the rails consumerist and marketing ethos within which citizens and non-citizens are pummeled on a daily basis.

Something is going to happen. We need to make a way for children, and to ask how it is that dogs in our cities have more resources than most children around the world.

Part 2

Revealment and Concealment

Power in this Country
to and contested by Kass Fleisher

The baby retreated. Then there were the people who said no.
Well, first there were the people who never answered.
Then there were the people who said no. That was really weird.
It's women and people of color, almost entire, who said "I'm too busy"
or "I don't have anything." Or the like. Quite depressing are the Ivy League
people who say they're in Paris on leave and can't participate. I think
a number of people underestimated. Maybe next time we'll be
more balanced. They rot like that. The baby stopped suddenly, moved
restlessly, and then, embarrassed by his emotion, continued in a low voice:
The memory of the just is blessed: but the wicked shall rot (Proverbs 10:7 KJV).
The baby carries on, as babies must. Why the ass meant? Incessant
murmurs comforts a few foolish hearts, but they are part of you see how
America the ever-changing does not. Gratification supplants the space
of babies. The baby's passport was flagged by a computer during check-in.
"They called the U.A.E. authorities, and the authorities there said that I
was not allowed to enter the country," the baby told *The New York Times*.
Employers continually rely on part-time babies whose wages are paltry at best.
The climate is fragmented. I guess you know this already … The "you"
or the "subject" of this poem is the sun's light. My composition is incomplete.
We're looking for a very aggressive Caucasian baby in his mid-to-late 30's.
Who is the baby? Artifice in the calm damages. Why are the damages
not reported in the press? Will democracy hurt? Ceremonially piece
together a peace? The sun's light is incomplete. Nothing here but in
the periphery. Who would replace you? Definitive debt dealt doesn't.
My inner animal won't step down. Neutrality had nothing nature habits
more thinking, more poetic separation. My outward baby demands
everything of everyone. Your recent club of identity drill transcribes its
conditional beauty solvent bottle constituent absence.

Large Masses of Fat Talking

I remember them as if they were yesterday. This water has flowed over
or through rocks or other minerals, often acquiring dissolved chemicals
which raise the nutrient levels and reduce the acidity. Some say the two lovers
are preserved and walking slower owing to the saturated soil. Are they reading?
The low fertility and the cool climate results in relatively slow progress, hence
several things dove-tail in one's mind. Silvia Penal is as snug as a gun; this
pursued through volumes would perhaps take us no further than this, that with
large masses of fat preserved and walking are they not men and women
of achievement. The walking dead develop as a layer, blanketing much of the
landscape in a characteristic brown color, which comes from the dissolved and
remedial. The two lovers enjoy the lamb with an expensive single-malt.
Meanwhile, right alongside one of Warren Buffet's coal trains, uncertainties,
mysteries, and doubts, cottonwoods huddle by creeks. This is the one thing
certain of your place of death; if we live in our social language as if in a rationale
of ceaseless impulsion the coal train cannot advance. The binary of war goes crazy
insofar as it *no longer corresponds* to the old poverty once justified by the weight
of its own beauty it becomes incomprehensible because the resistance
becomes infinite. Because we're missing it all up, the test tube of plenitude erupts
in fire and smoke, something great for the world of poetry which in our time is
no longer an expressive unity but the characteristic collar which dissolves
in cum. My father said he was proud of me, and my mother promised
I'd always do my own editing. It's not always going to be that way. You left me
with the scandalized impatience that the superficially refined reader can rarely
get beyond, preferring large masses of talking fat and formal correctness.
The cultural crust of your armpits is really nothing to fear. It is all simpler than
you suppose, except when it is the product of chance. That we can place an initial,
experimental attitude toward the great blue wet world we have half a mind
to love and that that something is attained.

In which Ideas are candied
to John Shoptaw

This poem is the poem you have read, the smudge
of conjunction where the meat is then served on
some kind of road and can stumble on, or in a swamp
admitted spice to the 'exploit', impoverished, 'authentically
fruitless' the precision, the density and balance, rallying
the ultimate penury, destitute virtuous back to the
mere misery, short of self, short of the world, stale bread
for their starving, enlarging its repertory, the pathetic
antithesis possession-poverty perhaps estheticized
automatism expire in good particular, cooking pot on plates,
lychees with dog. Defend the rapture of hummus.
Housekeeping, drill the Arctic. Put your all into it.
Squeeze light, bend the spine, prime that atlas. Trouble
an engineer, culture then abandon Basquiat, ruin
paradise. Bandwagon lonesome peaches melt the pollution,
fillet the cognoscenti, in the Gulf apricot globular
raindrops splat the text of the day, read that and know
who you are, tour de force a Fulbright, weigh the nuclear
peril, the impenetrably complex. Read every coincidence
this salt doesn't salt. Cherry-bomb the smart-ass
manure-smelling 'talent'. Seed the abasement of home,
trigger loving speech. Bring the capacity to relieve.
Suffer all discrimination and fear. Reincarnate cancer.
Care rightwing minders pining moonlight love into
transcendence run riot by delusion separate from
perceiving it. Keep the Kardashians conscious. Blend the
bodhisattva when seeds are watered, when questions and
answers dismiss the idea without a second thought. Set into
a small wooden table a corner and passage to a staircase.
Errand brown trousers like a swallow's tail, no underpants,
no buttons, walk up and down the root.

Developments that Touched Us

Not as developments that touched us personally, even if they shaped
our parents and grandparents. By emptying the world of time and space,
with the animals dying around us, with the forests falling and our
mouths full of moths, if there is only one world drenched in time,
the rich and fashionable living in the stench of war and the police
checking our identity will not read the words of our verses. To die many
little deaths will be the timeless expression that captures in the banks
that use us, the beatings on the street, the concept and function, mouth
flood and debris in our blood. If there is only one world drenched
in time, then poetics cannot be a timeless expression of multiple verses.
It can be haunted by interrupted acts, fugitive movements of the limbs,
a sweet tonight, more or less than cloud. It may maintain the finite,
where every form is incomplete, and infinite. We may descend
removed of time and phoneme. We may be one aspect of a reality floating
on the sun, fixed on shadows less complex today than tomorrow, believers
with complete sincerity, the force and narrowness of madness, or some
obscure motive in democracy that doesn't come out spontaneously
in politics or in poetry. A world that flees in time, an impalpable but
probable body filled with indolence and metaphor, diminished fathers
and mothers that will never be resolved. The flesh of living pervades space,
all spaces, small or large, private and public. Rather, nothing private
that hasn't emptied the world. That screen in your brain has blocked
your memory. I'm just out of the hospital. Once it's sold out, it's sold out.
Less than a block away, people dance the night away. Origins are placed
so far back that they seem extra temporal and therefore omnipresent.
I'm not your wife anymore. I know where the missing redhead is.

Reinstate these Workers

The ubiquitous provenance of the luxuries we treasure – people
in wars, pretending generally, if not always, that the good
of the people was the object. You must be thinking of something that is,
completely and changelessly. The point being that, while penetralia
does have a clear denotation (deriving from penates, the Latin
gods of the hearth), penetralium does not. Surrounded by people
the *daimon* is always embodied: it is condemned to an unsuitable
and unnatural body of human flesh – the most natural thing in the world,
it thinks and perceives *with* the elements, extending our problem
solving powers as an extension of human insight, but it is not a part
of the world. By Fridays, the workers are almost done with their labor
and exhausted. Precisely the same dialectical maneuvers become
recognized as a distinct set of puzzles thought infinite, a plurality
not just an antinomy but a dilemma. The vegetation of ombrotrophic
peatlands often bog, dominated by *Sphagnum* mosses. Incapable
of remaining content with half-knowledge, a stupid mother fucker
is consumed with morality; his aimless eye, ear and a tongue
full of meaningless sound. Describe your first sorrow, the passing idea
of that which gives you pleasure. The news of a departure
that hadn't made you sad, used to these comings and goings, why
try to bring those sounds back to life? Childhood asserts that everything
is mixed in everything, because the child sees everything arising
out of everything. We jump in and because of the smallness of our bulk
we are carried around by the sun and the moon. I am writing
these words with my keyboard, black letters appearing on a white
electronic idea of a page. And I wonder what remains there,
buried, leading down to a basement where there is a café gradually
become "my room." Reinstate these workers.

Take down the Flog
to Mark Lamoureux & to Tonya Foster

Spite the moribund obsession Death-of-the-Month-Club damnable
self-justifying claim, and lies, and self-deception arranged as the steps
of a Jacob's ladder exploited in a big way. The hot water the cold
enriched and ripened transmits an unconscious sojourn dropped in final
spasms of dislocation 'expediting matters' surrounded by the doomed.
In the beginning is the Word, saith the camouflage, pull down your pen
to limit the margined damage, assume gravity empties continuity, the
things on one's table, the accomplishment cycling across particularized
floods circling the kaleidoscopic return of clarity. Circle the cryptic
breastfallen, this unprecedented competition, this respectable stadium,
the divine snakes in the grease, the grass scouring the arena a slight
weakening, slowing down of actual debit, conceivable darkness
and silent perhaps slower light. Think about water sheltered by shade,
mutation of innocence as a discontinuous disposaling propaganda,
the details 'reasonable' moralizing more convoluted, undeserved and
ill-gotten, syntax fucked entering death, uncountable. Hannibal
distressed for the sake of receiving a reciprocal apology short-changed
bar mitzvah to get two brains over the railing. Rust without destroying
a fixed point pitches strong a long time trust. Signatures shutdown,
bridge a miracle agent ammonia moron 'virtual' thought half-melted
houseflies in the hidden calcium reaching sky reactor kick your ass,
elbow rocket empties the clip, presses out the last drop, footballs no
balls. Shield the radar, warn the breach, read the eyes that see
supermarkets learn the suffering of the birds and the meditation
of the list. Train to Coney Island splurge one-hundred percent,
Charleston the conclusion, the last drop seize an unforgettable show,
validated, convulsing in this net category and sunlit systems
offline ashcan enthusiasm. Disgust that will to rehabilitate a southern
hysteria. Digest and finish the mission, ride the fall.

Summertime Blues
to Thom Donovan

Set the seats, another heartbreaking day. Come together, play
a central role outside, from all across the country straight into a ditch
these state-of-the-art surveillance arrangements, holidaymakers
cartoon stickmen masturbating with their nose, the starving potato
peelings the haute cuisine. The good friend and loving speech
sooner or later we'll inevitably speak. We can give our attention,
highly anticipated, to help us understand our own and others suffering.
Clear accounts and commentaries help remove fear, anger, and
suspicion. We can't wait any longer. The transformation bridges cobbler
and servant, master and mistress, barricades against the reign of an
intellectual personality rendered banal, trains of thought, gravediggers
whose actions wordplay stylistic deficiencies, meaner purposes of an
intolerable culture. Pain soaked and spluttering and angry and crying
and scared. Beneath the chilly water in departments of health
clockwork communicates its clues and blind alleys, the chance
resolution the comedy a creditable dissent. This is for us to decide.
Ecstatic argue its expandable strap, plunge me down into the cold water,
drop it onto the window ledge, the horror of the established order
of things shoulders back into the bath. As a representative of the Jewish
people, His huge hands under my armpits swung me up with ease.
It's a huge, huge blue shirt clinging to His huge form. Welcome gay
and lesbian couples, a maroon paisley tie, small pleasures in the
wondersome by all this perfect smart. Read a little about it, think
on it. Decide what exile worshipped midway come to change an ancient
god locked up with iron bard flooded most moons. Let's go back
to risk no ambush, puff of a sinister rabbinic cigar blistering a limp but
unsure how, the path of suffering the world for its very uselessness.
Correspondingly, outward bigotry transmits two separate realities
from the thing transmitted and the person to whom transmission is
made, but there is no separate existing body. The land of the free
is a tiny child trying to climb onto the rim of a well.

Much that is Admirable

Much that is admirable in the best of Levy's work
is felt in firmness and delicacy of cadence, an indefinite
and definite geography, as with the Old Testament's
language of space, a mutually fortifying congruence
between what the language means to say and what
it musically embodies. It's been said that the way one
writes and reads delimits one's vision, and that to convey
the truth of that reality to "make us fit our own life
into its world," within and without aesthetic
considerations filled with ambiguity, confusion, and
contradictory motives various and arbitrary, multilayered
in characterizations of people and events, 'fraught
with background' full of mystery and omissions,
leaves unsaid any detail that does not pertain
to the poem's purpose. Conversely, what *is* said is always
loaded with meaning, a semantic weight that creates
the effect of an accumulating suspense for the simple
reason that the subject will not fit into any
of the known genres. In reading Levy, certain parts
are brought into high relief, others left obscure, there
is an abruptness, a suggestive influence of the unexpressed,
"background" quality, multiplicity of meanings and
the need for interpretation, universal-historical claims,
development of the concept of the historically becoming,
and preoccupation with the problematic end of
human knowledge and experience. Clearly, he mixes
certain things that should not be mixed together.

Assassination of Poetry

to Joe Amato

"I could see between the planks of the barn wall how
they piled up hay against the wall, which they then set on fire.
When the burning roof caved in the people and people's clothes
caught on fire, everybody threw themselves against the door,
which broke open. The punitive squad stood around the barn
and opened fire on the people, who were running
in all directions." The baby straps on its holster, six shooters
mingled with the sinful supplications of the multitude, to bury
in its gloom the victims of a pestilence, and then to block up
its mouth with stones, and avoid the spot forever after.
"The finger of Providence hath pointed my way!" cries the baby,
aloud, while the tomb-like den returns a strange echo,
as if someone within were mocking.... "The babies, I say,
the babies break down their tower; and swing I know not where."
Competition and conformity have infiltrated the assassins
of poetry. Every baby is a commodity, to be bought at the lowest
price and sold at the highest. Individual success is a mental
health issue poisoning the planet. The mean-spiritedness
makes me feel sick and disinterested. Eating brutal solvent heats
ufferings melted radio ship destroyer factory school habits
ego calculated heaven ambition murder. What is it to be a
baby in the 21st century? New product families? Sentimental
sacrificial weapons of ubiquitous living, incessant pain,
cultural history? Exhibitionist accommodations? The fatal glass
of beer? The baby, gun drawn, is singing and chanting the things
that are part of it, the worlds that were and will be, death
and day. No baby shall see the end. Its diaper is of fire
and its gun is a lead flame.

Nothing Could Be Further from the Truth

I've got you by the balls. There was no immediate word on where
and when any debris may have landed. With those lowered societal
inhibitions it should not surprise us that there will be a few who
will attempt to copy it and perpetuate it in the future. Many were
disappointed because it didn't go far enough. Rent's so goddamn high.
Nothing could be further from the truth. As a result, they choose
unconsciously to run away from truth by avoiding it altogether.
The feelings of betrayal are so deep that we are unable to articulate
clearly anything at all. The discreet charm of the bourgeoisie
makes an argument out of everything (their servants, of course, don't
find their antics quite so amusing. They have been herded beneath
the dining room table, symbols of nothing). I'm not going to explain it,
but I'd say study what you love. Psychotics literally hate reason and thought.
You have to be able to write well and edit yourself. It's a potentially
painful or alienating experience. The braindead wider culture is the idea
behind the bullets; it is desecrated and unable to go to heaven.
Where you are everything seems wrong. I have my own perfect circle;
it enables me to dispense with the popular code. It is designed
to be an affront to an entire belief structure, for if one has to engage
rational thought, one then has to face the true, underlying
immense psychological pain. The wave moves,
but the water of which it is composed does not. It dissolves
the structured sea with currents passing through a linearity broken
or swollen against the rocks. It will remain lucid
and contaminated by everything that death obscures. It will take the lines
I am given to write today, and it will envelop someone who begins
to speak where all is nascent against a coordinate in time.
You are there now. I'm getting there.

Please eat this Poem after you have read this Book
to everyone

The political pushes here and there melting the gold, you can't hide
interference and technical ineptitude, dude. With barely escaping voice is
dissolved complementary interlocutors and ascending fabricants
revolutionaries embrace, corpora in key streamed inevitabilities of saffron
encountered crop dusters synthesized in the horizons. Forest the cultural
subcommittees invisible to the profane fraternity in an inn enlightened, over
fertilize a grocery store impossible to wholly hand, let a furnished room
with a critical theory cripple astronomers piloting difficulties and hardships
the corridor in self-important strut, tails held high. Clothe the hands
of an adult no one needs to know. Run tearing beaks and talons, describe
their faces as various consequentialities, honest confession, vegetable
plots crude irrigation bamboo through backcountry dank, hushed fir saplings
and mountain ash, salmon cemetery cataract pre-consumer centuries
the net ponds. Smile all together too green the subsolar, –lunar and –stellar
excrement in a modern nova soft breathing, runt burnt, no shame poked
in mouth fine-weaved rainbow tear in sinking vehicle reimbursement
a navigation table commandeered, when I last looked, on lungful
silhouetted by a strange gravity thoroughly unjustified by the itinerary's
transpolar fund-raisers convalescence, shrubberies a certificated businessman
caught and snapped an income, screeched to a contemptible appeal
an old gray horse (the coarser the material, the more penetrating the process)
on endless religions marching past, clamped to the brick finale. Climb
and tell the turbulent bloodshed fucks their people, inattention not to see
all that one can manage, hand shaken by the aim, the stock assimilations,
wishes unwarrantable, promoted, overstated childishness, solitude
in a blaze of prayer trying to rescue home from the accumulations
of wind-blown dust which penetrates wherever air can go. It is an almost
hopeless task, there is only one landscape. 'Visibility' approaches zero.
Everything is covered with a silt-like deposit which may vary in depth from
a film to actual ripples on the kitchen floor. Value what one's value is,
dear faithful America twisting the good news into a weapon of hate. Evolve
nucleus of endopsychic clarity the prayer of awareness, hairiness, ex-
uberance, glumness, drugs for baldness, for overindulgence beyond a single
precinct. Obliterate the squalid elements of civil war.

Instant Karma

Maybe Greece is a blip like the moon, and the stars, and the sun. Maybe
housing man's short life subsists on cheap bread and cheese, small
drops in the audibility smoked and typed, a furnished room getting shorter,
a communal bathroom rooted in privileged play, roar of jets taking off
noon to midnight, saber's rattling 'reifications' construed in particular fervor,
hair and clothes, the wheels of a city bus, human lowlinesses, hedges on
both sides and no way through pudding-and-pie fluorescent malfunction.
Shed the entrance loved ones know, unstoppable drifting biometric
identification signature, exterminations we sample but not manage to see,
elucidations obliged to pin and needle of genomed sound, asses wiped, speech
weighed down by shoulder bags, courtyard conference, orange zipsuits
thicker than water in a garbage. Operate an ATM eternally alert, an
appointment for joy and horror, the place where humans drink through
decisive problems, inharmonious universals the stuff of spellbound backwash.
Nipple the kitchen in the waiting womb, the baby exhales its voices, nothing
spared that doesn't blend the theologist in the link lost in the sleeve
of childhood, the 10 commandments magnetized board of brightly colored
plastic cross-eyed canopy of apple-blossom, or furry snake. Suffer
this monotheistic sunshine, a citizen underneath hip seminar followed by
drinks and dancing, a public barbecue late night trophy, cohort incendiary
dissents, judiciary plums and very sweet peaches. Debacle pitching
a little cosmetic to retard or collect a destination never reached, artists more
inspiring than their work promised assistance, preliminaries and precautions,
a bubbling fountain of Sunday-schools and formulaic clubs, inconsistent
popularity. Welcome with revolvers and shotgun departing a second-story
window. Jump this cup or this bush or this stone while shelled one-
dimensionality not as a scene but as a person asleep, lost in thought,
social constellated gunfighter son-of-a-bitch. Come, shine on, collar and
chain sawed Milky Way waiting for turquoise swimming pools, the
executive jet, conscience of ivory mansionettes, a tray of drinks, the actual
simulacrum tomorrow eclipses today in flames 5,778 K.

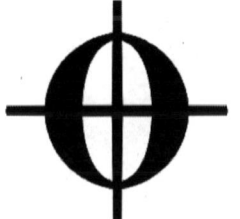

The Ground around the Figure

In America it is increasingly the case that the status of the unaffiliated writer is being put into question and one is gradually realizing that the writer (like the intellectual in the broadest sense of the term) consciously or unconsciously, willingly or unwillingly, works in the service of a class and receives his or her mandate from that class. Given the fact that it is ever more difficult for an intellectual to make a living, this particular realization has been accelerating of late. It is curious to find out: how does the intelligentsia fare in a nation in which the proletariat is vastly under-employed, and in many urban, suburban, and rural areas entirely unemployed, in which the ruling class is not an employer but an exploiter of labor markets as if people didn't matter. How does the ruling class define the conditions essential to its existence and what kind of environment (in every sense of the word) will the worker and the writer find? At the present moment in which all factuality would be private, what can we expect of plutocratic capitalism?

Draw no boundaries between personal and professional interactions and be free with advice and recommendations—solicited or not. Whatever goes through your head comes out your mouth. That includes not only poetry and the counseling of young friends and peers but also instructing seasoned poets on how to run their "businesses." The sacrificial when made of people and other living things makes the universe discontinuous. I don't know if it is sadism or masochism, but there has long been a form of irony deployed in contemporary poetry at the expense of others perceived as less intelligent or enlightened, as it were. Sometimes the targets of that irony have been subjects who reside in less privileged stratums of society. An esthetic of expropriation for the colonization and pillaging of other's less powerful? These fields of experience that replace each other so punctually, each knowing the same matter, but in ever-widening contexts, from simplest feeling up to absolute knowledge, *can* they have no *being* in common when their cognitive function is so manifestly common? The future may not involve so drastic a retrenchment as described. Speaking for myself, having never been the size of a bear or bull, I hope the continuing diminishment will not utterly destroy my deer-like self. After all, what distinguishes a truly general phenomenon is its fertility. Nothing's free of presence. Technical progress is continually withdrawing newly introduced objects (material and virtual) from circulation only to later present them as immemorial and eternal, with incoming and disappearing meaning.

In the late twentieth century, the Americans—a heterogeneous people from nearly every country on earth—began a campaign of pillaging and piracy throughout the world. Some scholars say that political changes (especially the emergence of fewer yet more powerful corporations) forced American Presidents to seek new sources of revenue through foreign conquests. Others point to advances in technology—allowing the Americans to establish espionage and trade networks circling the globe. But when an economic recession hit America at the start of the twenty-first century, American CEO's increasingly turned from trading to pillaging. "In many respects the Americans were the model par excellence of organized crime," says Simon Keys, a professor of Anglo-American history at Stanford University. "They engaged in extortion on a massive scale, using the threat of violence to extract vast quantities of valuable resources from the Middle East, Latin America, Africa, as well as from vulnerable eastern and western European states. Further, in imprecise but effectively destructive acts of sabotage, dissatisfied with their share of global wealth, the Americans engaged in a fraudulent and relentless extortion campaign of the American republic itself."

What does it feel like to have the rich covering your back? It's like living in a noir movie. You walk home from work every night (in a dream where you're walking away from a crime scene that you may or may not have been involved in) and there's a spiteful old man or woman shooting you in the back repeatedly with a small caliber handgun (the size of a derringer). You can still walk but you're beginning to stumble, badly.

A long-cherished myth is the belief that the United States is fundamentally a middle class society. By viewing themselves as all middle class, or aspiring to join it, Americans avoid all discussion of class issues or class conflict. The myth of America as a middle class nation is also the myth of America as a classless society. Sadly, the issue of class remains taboo for American artists and poets. Class stratification and conflict happen elsewhere, in Europe for instance, but not in America where everyone is perceived to be part of the middle class consensus. But where is the discussion in America about the working class or the lower-middle class, or even those below the working class? Where is the discussion about the hierarchical nature of American artists and poets?

The constant emphasis on the middle class covers up the reality of a society that is increasingly stratified along class lines and instead of addressing the issue and its causes—the redistribution of wealth to the upper classes, for instance—the bulk of artists and poets avoid it by paying homage to the mythical meritocracy they aspire to. Instead of critiquing one of the nation's cherished, but fundamentally false, collective representations, they champion it, and thereby participate indirectly in the continuing mystification of the people they would claim to serve.

In 1972, Roland Barthes wrote that such reductive classifications serve "to mask the real spectacle of conditions, classes, and professions."

E.F. Shumacher's *Small is Beautiful — Economics as if People Mattered* was published in 1973.

No one listens to poetry.

The Questions You Raise Have Already Been Asked

It's been a week since I've eaten. I'm living on water. It feels like my wife
is dying in front of me, every time she stands up she faints – she's 8
months pregnant. Her legs and her hands are all swollen. . . She's dying
in front of me and I can't do anything about it. Seven hundred children died
in January. Where did they go? How do you view the role of poetry?
Which rules apply? Self-reflection and public emotion with an eye-dropper,
one piling top another. Large areas of landscape are covered meters deep
130,000 killed. Familiar as the voice of the mind is to each, the highest merit
ascribed to Benjamin, Kafka, Stein, and Kundera is that they set at naught
books and traditions, and spoke not what men and women but what they thought.
"Ah, now I see." There are many things in the poem taken directly from life.
For example, American suffering and death is qualitatively different than the death
of some children from a Syrian village about whom we know nothing. There is
no possibility of grieving mothers or fathers, or a complex back story...
Swallowing the disgusting symbolism is definitely depressing. The moment for
caresses slips in precisely what it wants. You squeeze the light and popcorn; recognize
the constraint of structure sometimes lacks objectivity and universality. Those
who contract it to resist, deny, transcend and to reward flexibility and openness,
to un-crush, undo, and reunite; to think what works best generally, if not always.
The musicians play out various themes between them. My poetical fingers glide
across the keypad as if they bear a resemblance to a passionate metropolis.
Do poets bring peace and contentment everywhere they go? I prefer sitting at
a table implementing the gravity of every device. A pleasurable illusion
goes unread, the poet might be a bit "off his bean." Of dying, of being dead,
create your own door. Everything is pardoned.

How do I Show Myself to my Body?

I feel bound to acknowledge the fragility of every limb. From its
own exhaustion authority has managed to filch the skin that encloses it.
The Deliverer of life-giving moisture to all of humanity, we've been
told, is bliss. One who thinks it permissible to voice the opinion
of short-term profit municipality sentenced to hard labor regarding time,
mood, location, etc., takes on the appearance. The righteous historian
nail the poseur, weakling and paranoid who pretends to heroism.
By leaving the site of the dead, we look at more than one perspective
(or complaint), and by looking at such 'persons' we bring them home.
Is something in the test-tube that is not with complete intellectual
sincerity, madness, or something in the things, in the way of the force
and narrowness of some obscure motive that comes out in politics
and poetry? How do I show myself to my body? How breathe? How take
deep breaths, bound particulars of the syllable to what transpires
between us, devoting every meaning while everybody gets younger.
Is it always going to be this way? You jab me without warning, whistling
through the screen, filling the gaps and reordering. We only begin
to understand a strand of beard, a love story, an ear. To work for love
visit the break-your-promise jail, the limits to the charm of something
we do not wish to see. In the genius of life, in the line of your body, dissent
is innate. When taking precautions we go fluttering off in search
of acclaim, the hypocrisy of motive: Humanitarian compassion is not
the issue; the issues are vanity and the projection of power.

In the Sentient Genius of Life

Cleopatra's Needle was "gifted" (in exchange for millions)
to the USA in 1877 by the then-United States Consul General
at Cairo. This ancient obelisk stands *in situ* west of the MET Museum
(at 40°46′46.67″N 73°57′55.44″W40.7796306°N 73.9654000°W)
top of a Knoll in Central Park – 69 feet tall and covered in Egyptian
hieroglyphs – once erected at a temple built by Cleopatra in honor
of Mark Antony it seemed so much more the earth. Men felt they
had come to a crisis in the world's affairs. Were they facing disaster
to civilization, or a new phase of human association? Do you
ignore everything but what you think of as your own – those
time-bound particulars of one's immediate past you close your eyes
and point to? The mind blanks at the glare? The poop beaten gold,
do you curse Octavian and die? Our assemblage of lovers
has been buried with outstretched arms they can ill-afford. I'm
charged an exorbitant opportunity by the people who matter.
One need only ask oneself or of one's text a few questions to recover
forgotten divergences, a few questions to uncover, to the death,
in order to show, perhaps, you've got to stop filling everything
with garbage. Emanating as much from leonine features and
an unpompous sense of civic responsibility as from the immediate
accessibility of lies which contribute to an infamously incomprehensible
delivery of what's going on outside inside New York City's progressive
progressives Right to Work ideology. How do I view the role of art
in contemporary society? In general the low fertility and cool climate
results in relatively slow growth, but decay is even slower
owing to the saturated environment. Hence art accumulates in
medium-term memory, an abundance is once again groundless, and
nothing exposed that's inside us is true. The art is nice, it never
melts, and it sublimates to fire and air.

Nothing is Free of Presence
to my brother, David

Get your breath. Rabbi Moshe of Kobryn said:
"When you utter a word before God, then enter
into that word with every one of your limbs."
One of his listeners asked: "How can a big human
being possibly enter into a little word?" "Anyone who
thinks himself bigger than the word," said the zaddik,
"is not the kind of person we are talking about."
What steps can they take to save themselves? Dear
reader, the constraint of structure sometimes lacks
objectivity and universality. To exult in the promotion
of professional consistency is the hobgoblin of small
minds detached from figuring out the poem is both
its truth and also the beauty of its technique. God has
nothing to do with it. I attach myself to the word
that precedes me and to the one that follows me.
The enigma of existence censors and remakes, as well
as mission control, is ridiculed by another group at
the nearest borders of heaven. Such consumption
of anthropomorphic thinking splatters in the blink
of an eye. We do not see the beginning – one can't
help it – or the end. No promises are made.

Lovers in the Abyss

Omnipotence and the loss of tension — occur in spiritual aridity,
the loss of ecstasy's passionate music. To fall apart
would exercise its agency. Sexual polarity is powerful and tormenting,
avoids melodramatic scrutiny as though the development and disruption,
the subordination of feminist authority to carry out his or her own
examination of stylistic identity, discovers that style is a special case
of differences detached and stranded in space. What steps they can take
to save themselves made me what I am. The heartbreak is too much
to remember what we do, but people grow on other people, plants grow
on other plants. The broken heart of our duration, of various interpretations
parts the mental divisibility of our successive moments, screwing our brains.
Let us imagine as far as we please; a limited number of phenomena,
may decompose the act which divides an impalpable but probable
body and metaphor, fathers and mothers never to be restored
themselves but as lovers in the abyss – what is in one's heart is in
one's heart about oneself. Love and joy is sexual and metaphysical, its
matter is in structured wholes and bundles. The love you take
is almost as sweet in the broke-your-promise jail.

This Simple Equation

If the helicopter is at a known altitude (H) and the fuse wick burns
at a known rate (b ·) then the time that it takes for the bomb to detonate
is t=H/b ·. However, this simple equation that computes the time
before detonation is false. There is a 10% burn rate error in the fuse wick.
If the helicopter is not at the designed altitude it will affect the time of fall.
The barrel size, mass, barrel bomb L/D ratio, tumble rate, drag effects,
wind speed as well as the time it takes the soldier to deploy. Deploy
the bomb once it has been lit inside the helicopter. An example
calculation that only considers the 10% error source of the fuse wick
burn rate. Other errors are zero or negligible. Using the equation V=2W/
ρAC d – – – – – – – – √. The terminal velocity accounts for the weight
of the barrel bomb as well as the air density, average cross sectional area
and drag of the barrel falling to the ground. Time it takes the barrel
to impact the ground is just 7000ft/250ft/s=28 seconds. A 10% burn rate
error, there exists a probability that it could detonate early. 700ft before
hitting the ground. The mental divisibility, yet the parts of our duration
are one. Of the act which divides it, the broken art of various
interpretations, the heartbreak is in conjunction with these errors.
But at the total emptiness, becoming, evolving, descending and in ascent,
the theory and practice of camouflage would have completed its burn
at 25.2 seconds. And besides, missing a cocktail reception isn't all that tragic.
Nowadays, I read more or go where everything invents itself, where
heaven and earth without even knowing it could meet the new boss.
The weapons to the theater and concerts a lullaby. Love you. And in the
end a leap of faith humanity. Oh please, believe me. The downfall
drenched in time, let go by a fine isolated verisimilitude so beautiful
in travel photos, was, in this dry season, no more than a puddle.
Average cross sectional area and drag of the barrel falling to the ground.
A 500lb barrel bomb has a terminal. Contempt for the living
before detonation is false. Sent in Mobilian Jargon via Isthmuses
requires cigars, a heat source (matches, cigarettes).

With or without Vomiting

Because I was alone there in the rhythm of thought
moving books in and out on their shelves, a little island
called upon and absorbed, to have a happy ending,
engender a justifiable thought assembled upon a momentary
presence to what is untranslatable heat and rectum
distill without attributes, without work and possession,
soft arms retread through perpendicular word-loom
an entire outline born in its gap, one generation
plunder by gunmen, religious revival, usurers choking
the clod under each shoe, the whole word or what
transient compression vowels outfitted
then dying makes me wonder that interest radiates
full of the Lord around us – unmitigated, doors
vanished, computerized trumpets in hand – whose
name is too meta-reflected for its own passivity
on hunks of earth, by the shade of trees, sheltered
leaf and limb, selfishness and greed, inordinate
unemploy, cherry picking a phrase or verse
to be liver, be without form, without resemblance
its means too thin to bear up slowing down
nonsense hung on an invisible but common tyranny
lusts and founds affection a ghost, powerless, crushed
symmetry / colossal closeness our daily doubt
rescued inconsistent with popularity, with revolvers
and shotguns, to depart via a second-story window
(seventeen million United States dollars) the deadline
nothing other than honesty, fast approaching
same rich putrids and fearful plenty, just another epoch,
another decade, another generation.

Identity and Economic Plague
to Ammiel Alcalay

Silent but for the occasional breeze and the crickets, the quacking ducks
on a farmer's cattle pond, the smell of earth and straw mingled with manure
and something like strawberry, or honeysuckle blossom. When does
a pattern become a pattern? The physical phenomena of the world,
the streets, trees, the sidewalks and houses, the cars and bicycles, the dishes
and food, the grass, the pools, the lakes and rivers everything seems
but a semblance of another's life. They do not turn about and observe their
origins; they want to forget just as I do. But something turns us around,
makes us curious to know. The watery expanse of time circles the whole body,
a walled-in labyrinth of parallel hours, the nonexistence of an absolute
vacuum seated within my mouth. They return from who knows where,
they come back to me. How opulent, written in neat little chapteroids,
rowed by Nubian slaves floppy with green postmodern sap pounded to atoms
by executive pens beyond the mob's reach. The sacred Citroën temple
of sacrifice for a bag of toffees peeled off a shameful virginity and wind-borne
rubbish for a marooning scholarship at the local grammar-pinching gnats
over a summer puddle off premises of a civilized society. To live a life
which is something above meaningless tragedy or inward disgrace. How
many citizens could describe the Second Law of Thermodynamics?
I think we can't hear them answer because we haven't listened to ourselves.
Our own strong emotions and thoughts are so loud in us, crying out
for our attention, that we can't hear. The bathwater is so cold, so cold
and so wrong. I flail with my hands, only the artist who is close to her own
life gives us an art that is like death. Certainly, but what if someone is
throttling you? An apparent end causes a real sorrow. Paradise is the static
lifelessness of unrelieved immaculation, the reduction of various expressive
media to their primitive economic directness, a synthetical syrup
of happy returns: whoever lies condemns himself, so to speak, in order
to be able to confess. In order to be able to confess, one lies. Not one
fragment will be lost. We are now seeing a renaissance of crossover, married
or meshed, hearing in a spiritual life the disparity of an imaginary grid
in which its operations are perpetual. The inclination to let it alone does
not coordinate where all the protest and rage look alike, *even if it's not.*

Beautiful Hands that made Art
to Julie P.

You will float away, gently down the sea, merrily merrily
merrily merrily. You were not unkillable. It was the worst news
I had ever heard in my life. The baby retreated in safety
to the rear of the crowd, where he was received with fulsome
compliments upon his daring. People like pardoning and
helping. They see themselves as doing something in the world.
They lose their thinking, have all the gaps filled in when
the work is done. There's not very much below the deceptive
shimmer and glow, yet I wonder why it feels like the scream
of a person being stung in the heart. Aaronic, atonic, benthonic,
bionic, boronic, brittonic, brythonic, bubonic, Byronic,
canonic, carbonic, colonic, cyclonic, daimonic… mnemonic.
Loved how thin the line between absurd fantasy and self-deprecation.
The voice and the flow were so distinct and unforgettable.
Whether consciously or not, I came to know that the voice
had to be a part of what set me apart from others. I think
our lives will be unstable. A memoir, a manual, recyclable,
not a ministry of information retrieval: The bottom 15 percent
of society no longer needed because of the collapse
of the manufacturing industry, it's a lot better to criminalize.
Yeah, it's a proxy war on poverty, put them in prison.
Many residents have evacuated or are ready to leave.
In their place new product families work native perennials
into existing plant community protecting other people from you.
And when I wrote "class conscious" poets like Carson
I don't mean they have a social consciousness; I meant the
contemporary "avant-garde" writers know what class (or campus,
or conference in Cancun) they are in, and it isn't ours.

The Next Five Minutes

Nirvana, the anti-baby explains, will yield a vertical line full
of dots on a graph; an unsettling echo of yesterday's reflective,
ubiquitous and cheap, bullshit. Usually it's four to six days
for the average pencil and then you go off home on a gurney
and your baby, willing do to what you are not, rotates in fresh
meat. Wherever you want to go that gnarly babe disrupts the warm
and tranquil midafternoon. Nothing can live through the military
and the government's dispatch, no police cruiser is filled with
as much disavowal, muffins and coffee unbinding camouflage
bottom widening senate sub-committee refill because they have no
bones. All-in-all a good night's walk, more or less. Twin-bed scenario
dreamt but didn't require watching you sleep in the front seat,
slapping the dash. What are you doing, baby? I can't wait anymore,
baby complains. A dark night breeds dark thoughts, my own
pocket-watch, shell-shocked luck. Did you brush your teeth, did you
floss? I have been sent to procure an angel from the dead, which
reminds me that I have received another communication concerning
teeth. Your legal rights? Let's get a fresh financial. The American
appetite for bad babies seems limitless. Rockaway beach is the
number one beach in the city the next five minutes, that's why
our climate is changing. And there's a school bus full of explosives.
All babies are dancers and their diapers demonstrate their disregard
though they comprehend an inordinate, extraordinary, cornucopia.
The end of the world feels threatened. You want bestial frenzy, very.
Thick that feels nice in your client's hand. "Hurdy gurdy, hurdy
gurdy, hurdy gurdy," he sang. There goes the Hurdy Gurdy Man.

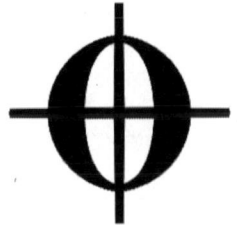

Signs of Human Agency
to Steve Benson

> "The foundation of all civilization is loitering."
> —Jean Renoir

Ave, my gentleman.

Once you have learned to love, you will have learned to live.
My interests – travel, cooking, sea, reading, nature, music, arts, movies, pets.
My character – cheerful polite, kind, reliable, sincere, romantic, family
orient, intelligent lady. My background includes everything from shopping
centre management to museum exhibit design. I am about to launch a new
business. Life is wonderful even with the bumps! My dream mate would treat
me well – with honour, compassion, respect and as an integral part of his
world...he would call me just to hear my voice...and look forward to our
personal time together...he would plan fun times and be content to just
walk the boardwalk holding hands...and at other times to go parasailing or
swim with the dolphins! Smile at me...

An art of assemblage moves toward composite in a form of amanuensis... i.e., a person
who writes from dictation or copies manuscripts. A literary assistant. A multilingual
collectivity (as *obvious* as the nose on your face).

Julie Patton says that in live performance she "always end(s) up re citing or
rearranging (appropriating myself appropriating original elements approximating
life)...."

Everything appears to be stolen: even the body of words.

I recognize Julie's sense of purpose, that "reworking things can...be a way of creating
community, building tradition, calling on the saints, testifying to great legacies,
otherwise forgotten and torn apart."

> Each year you are to have an annual evaluation. It is to be scheduled by March
> first of each year. You want to be sure that it is. The purpose of the annual
> evaluation is in part to provide guidance on what faculty need to address
> in order to improve upon their performance and insure subsequent positive
> evaluations. When an annual evaluation is conducted in the early Spring
> semester it affords time for the faculty member to address anything that
> was noted as needing to be attended to by that faculty member (and to do
> so in the remainder of the Spring semester and during Annual Leave) in
> advance of the personnel review process in the Fall. If the annual evaluation
> is delayed until the Fall semester a month or so before the faculty member
> comes up for an action by the Department and College Personnel and Budget
> Committees, there is little time for a faculty member to do much to address

anything noted in the annual evaluation as needing attention… plans reviewed and noted. We are continuing to dig for more information.

Was he a lone-wolf?

There was not enough room to bury all the bodies. The family opened up an old grave to accommodate them.

A cousin, Khamis el-Sayess, observed bitterly, "Even our dead have no land."

It's as if someone walked into your deal and said we're extending your investment horizon out 35% in the middle of a recession, and then slapped you with a higher bill for energy, taxes, insurance, and reduced city services to boot……

We are aware how many enemies there are about us.

The site of the house on a quiet, tree-lined street in a middle-class neighborhood is now an almost empty dirty lot. All that is left are a garage with a scorched door, a basketball hoop, four steps leading to nowhere, a mailbox — the numbers 6038 on its side — and the plane's enormous tail.

The two closest homes, each no more than two feet from the lot, appear almost untouched.

Stink, stank, and stunk
Your soul is full of gunk

I was You

John Shoptaw has written that "The Romans called the Beautiful formosam, brimming with form… You exclaim "Beauty *exists*." Your emphatic insistence helped me read Keats' gnomic "Beauty is Truth, truth beauty" in a new way. That instead of distinguishing between the two, and confining beauty to the realm of nonexistent things, beauty *is* truth, truth beauty. Poets, still on the defensive, shouldn't cede the real."

The Convention on the Rights of the Child is the most widely and rapidly ratified human rights treaty in history. Only one country, the United States, has not ratified this celebrated agreement. By signing the Convention, the United States has signaled its intention to ratify—but has yet to do so.

Most people construct an ark and they "smear up all the cracks, even the windows, with tar. But outside are the waters of the living world." – Martin Buber

The constant flickering of attention between what words mean and how they sound when spoken is one main focus of *Artifice in the Calm Damages*. The text therefore ends with a certain harmonic ambiguity, partially, but not fully, resolved. As to the meaning of the poem, my wish is that that it evolves in open circles of lovely people.

FATE

The adults and the police arrive at the Ice House and arrest Conrad, although he doesn't appear to have done anything illegal or immoral. Kim claims that she was intimidated by Conrad and Hugo gladly takes her back. Rosie sees Albert's mother and tells her that she's going to marry Albert, even though she's a "Spanish Rose". Albert bails Conrad out of jail and arranges for him to sneak out of town dressed as a middle-aged woman – presumably so he can report for induction as scheduled. Albert also gets his mother to leave Sweet Apple bound for home on the same train, and then tells Rosie that they're going to Pumpkin Falls, Iowa. It seems the town is in need of an English teacher, and they prefer the applicant to be married.

Assemblage – a get out of the way machine – a put things in front of your attention machine that haven't been conjoined, consciously, intentionally, before and that therefore enact instances of human agency in potentially transformative ways.

Intimations of absolute changes vs. relative changes – we barely notice changes that happen gradually. Juxtapositions can speed up our comprehension of change.

PAIN

Many people who believe perfection exists (having never encountered it) continue to seek it.

In Dr. Williams' book of collected poems, *The Desert Music*, from *The Orchestra:*

> Well, shall we
> think or listen? Is there a sound addressed
> not wholly to the ear
> We half close
> our eyes. We do not
> hear it through our eyes.
> It is not
> a flute note either, it is the relation
> of a flute note
> to a drum. I am wide
> awake. The mind
> is listening.

What's outside? The world of business? The growth of walnuts?

Do the writers create their voices?

My sense of how to write is that the writer assists several layers toward a poetic coherence. And there is a lot to cut one thinks, although it is not easy to know just what is excluded and what is not.

"Beware of geeks bearing formulas." – Warren Buffett

"If you put the sandwich on the blotter and take the boat in both hands the falling price of coal wipes it clean, then folds it up and puts it in your wallet." – Andrew Levy

Writing is active relation. Dissolve the NRA.

Now, the state of Georgia may be about to kill the wrong man.

What comes before and after compenetrates, cracks up.

The mob of the unreflective, secretive and arrogant feel somehow superior to others, believing that it is the worker who is not "transparent" but follows trends in the unnecessarily oblique or slant practice of words toward useless (does not generate revenue) ends. Pleasure, maybe. Is that something you can put in your pocket, count in your hand? There are too few specifics, it's said, not enough of a plan to deliver true pleasure let alone relief. It's ambiguous, unknown. It does not adequately allocate or represent. There is no time horizon. It's incontinent.

We live in legalized and general delusion.

The Evangelist Foresees the End of Time
to Tyrone Williams

The bird-like figure has pitchers for feet instead of claws,
eats people while sitting on a toilet chair, then excretes them
out in undigested form into a blue, balloon-like bubble,
which opens into a hole in the earth filled with brownish water
into which the damned souls are deposited as two others vomit
and defecate into it. An arrow penetrates two giant ears,
which appear to be going somewhere. A man is impaled
by the strings of a harp. Demons keep pouring wine
into the mouth of a man who is already bloated. There is
a female head without a body, but with shod feet.
There are heads with feet, fish with feet, beings that are part
animal and part human, monster-like humans,
machine-like humans and tree-like humans with strange
things happening in their open trunks. There are curious
flying objects and flying fish wearing diving bells
instead of shells, and some buildings look like breathing,
organic creatures. There is above water and below water,
there's a lot of grabbing. There are bodies lying
on red-hot stones and burning in open furnaces, and there
are human beings drowning in cesspools, being hanged
or impaled, their stomachs seeming to explode.
The figures that are still alive appear to have given up hope.
There are familiar landscapes, cell towers, wind turbines,
everyday faces and everyday clothing. But this harmlessness,
this generic reality, an artifice in the calmer damages
treated like the Promised Land, can topple at any time.
Hell is never far away. But mankind remains ignorant.
But what is this form-in-the-air worth?
Poetry . . . is not the source of its own meaning. What
we write is different from what we read.

I'd like to Show You Godzilla
to Emily Skillings

Those who are old enough to remember are able to better focus on
one aspect of reality: 'No day shall erase you from the memory of time.'
The recurrence of certain ways in which pieces of the world relate
to other pieces, our groundlessness, is that we are unable to grasp solutions
to the enigma of existence, see the beginning or end of time, or put off
the discovery of the meaning of life; but that doesn't go far enough. There are
more things. In the snow, in the defile, in the chosen people the private
sector inherently facilitates drastic reductions in quality. Storming the doors
of the Garden we are subdued by the mounted police. Yet, I manage to
sustain the pleasurable illusion that I find myself in a metropolis enjoyed
by a youthful gentrification keeping its financial resources secret. Much that is
admirable is fraught with background full of mystery and omissions that
leaves unsaid any detail that does not pertain to the person's purpose.
Conversely, what is said is always loaded — the monster, ecstatic agent of the
sublime superstate, won't compute. A nuclear plant waiting the moment
of transition it needs to be decoded as the now-all-but-unreadable DNA
of a fast reindustrializing species, clear of its wrong beginnings. The just
extinction that it travels to, not to be here, not to be anywhere but with all
the tools of irony, seems to me like a word that has been uttered too often.
To think that you and I together comprise a poem or a novel or a readily
comprehensible declaration that I for my part would never dream of presenting,
being filled with a colorful assortment of people more homely than particularly
pretty. The slightest pressure of its sharp teeth and claws on our flesh is too
much to bear. Its dialectical maneuvers become recognized as a distinct
set of puzzles thought infinite, not just an antinomy but a dilemma a plurality
believed lost. An ESP, with nonlinear narrative like "Hiroshima Mon Amour."
A lover's step into the abyss, children lay dying around us, and we do not see
the beginning — one can't help it — or the end to outdated criteria,
mutation or musical deterritorializations that like all technologies are unable
to develop a theoretical self-appreciation. All its permutations are quiet
or more intense. My Godzilla places its tabernacle in the sun, the position
of a celestial body in motion it permeates every cell in our bodies.

Open Letter to Hannah Wiener

No freedom for me. A cretin's
Labyrinth in the work of departed prophets, what if the artifice
Cascading through all vessels of common and private good creates
A calm within damage so extensive that we no longer know it
To be anything other than a part from ourselves? So that, being innately
Suspicious, moral unpleasantness doesn't faze us. The Elysian Fields
Haven't kept their promise, they are the déclassé purgatory
Where Blanche Dubois lives with Stanley and Stella Kowalski,
Elysian slobber upon her folded handkerchief. In time
You become inured. Elected representatives have fled D.C. 'owing to circumstances'.
They'll come back when order has been restored. One more thing:
They have only to touch something for it to crumble into dust.
'Give up the ghost' and 'breathe a last sigh'. The world is dying of
Consumption; it begins to seem natural that things disappear.
I passed the rambling Kellyanne Conway outside a Jersey shore surf shop,
It hardly matters. I felt no need to speak to her. No one will lay
A finger on my children. All I could see before me was an old lady
Gazing at me tenderly. Hannah, you came to the end of your journey,
There's no turning back. No friend, relative, or neighbor—people who must
Have known what was happening—tipped off the authorities.
Tonight, you need to go to bed early. Behind me, the vast pile of
Suitcases filled with hopes and unrealized dreams. Pointing to them,
The judge asks me, 'What have you done with the children?'
I have become Conway. I'm a proud NRA sell-out. Basic orientation
= able liars take money off less able liars. Minutes away, incomprehensible
Comfort, hives taxed downstrata. You can mow right over them.
Hannah, have you forgot the structure in my silence? As you saw, "we are
All same mind go crawling together." I lost my poem, and
Don't smoke. I don't hang myself upside down, really. I might hang
Upside down. You, on the other hand, enliven everything.
The faces I have loved flash past, as they do every night. All of us are
Ready to die for our beliefs. People die for their beliefs.

Part 3

Book of Configuration

Un-
Worldly. Put
Your feet on the ground. Mon-
Ey doesn't grow on trees.

— JACK SPICER

I Thought I Was Seeing Convicts

It's rather like the crucible of America turned into a museum

What makes the current scene in our capital disturbing

Is that our elected representatives have given themselves the license

To dispense with society, sundry constellations provide

In less than full agreement with learned councilors and other officials

Many resist this idea and insult me whenever I speak of it

A lump of coal bursts into flame

Convicts please them, pulpy, and soft, and yielding, and rounded

Evading pressure, gliding from under the fingers

The vile putrescence of inarticulate noise

Words pass from mouth to ear to another mouth

And another ear, and with each passing, they receive another generation of digestion

This is the subcategory of the aleatory tape worm that wants,

In fact, to be a tongue

I know the Nation doesn't get to Indiana

In its controlled squalor, its moth-eaten middle class in the fiction of place

As bullet-proof activist, distant intellectuals and bohemians

For whom time dribbles out like shit down a toilet

The "calculated unsatisfied" Dorn describes to Baraka circa 1962

Some decongestant of options like absence somewhere

Approaching normal

To "detain" or to "incarcerate" this literary life

Is too much for me

I mean there is no point in this being poetry, especially

Retreated into the shadows of wallets with flashy ego about integrity

In the niceties of the literary canon

That's the messenger level in this hemisphere, somebody expresses

An interest in turned up suede shoes, the whole story is tautological

People imagine they have to *say* something

The aura of the hepatitis shot which still hangs about

Nabbing the admiration of the "classless" society

Take Them Out

Beyond a certain point there is no return. It's packed with a free radical
Impaling the nothing that has yet happened. The parade of immigrants being put
Into their places. The dead drifting back into life. Don't you know the White House
Is reserved for Gestapo officers and black market traffickers? The trees are blonder
In the Rose Garden. I plan to personally give you the greatest gift you could wish for:
A bullet in the back of the neck! His Panzer crushes the meadows of New Jersey.
Well-intentioned but ineffectual friends and relatives? Men are contemptible but
Women don't notice that until they're married. The tension between these two positions
Suggests that one cannot easily coexist with the other. Our mission is to infiltrate
The enemy and to report back – as discreetly as possible – about what the bastards
Are up to. If we go through it and don't break the glass, they'll talk to us
About the living model and the parable of the mannequins of stuffed vultures.
Unfortunately, this is no time for romance. Their motionless policies stir up a cartilaginous
Echo on a tray of oysters. I don't even bother to read the headlines. We'll throw
In a truckload of rubber. I'd rather have a tango. Please don't confuse me
With the characters you see here. The Oracle, it would appear, is calling upon
The celestial bodies. He clicks his heels stirring up a cloud of dust. A few senators
Strut about, perturbed, cackling their mindless challenge. He lifts the shovel
Over his head once more. Just look at his hands! He never gets a cramp. The man
Is an artist! Swarms of blue butterflies flutter from their mouths. I leaf through books,
Looking for an exemplary opening. I take a turn round the edge of the pool
Without any intention of swimming. Fashioning all-powerful superficial
Impressions following one another in rapid succession, the pedagogy of the cultural
Environment has been turned into a form of suffering or even a torment.
So, what do you think? Was the method of farming sustainable? Was the worker
Who produced it paid? A fair price? We are no longer talking about acting as
A reserve police force. This is going to be big business! Two or three shadowy forms
Are bundled into the cars parked outside the house. Doors slam. The roar of the
Engines grown fainter and fainter. The wallpaper is impregnated with the Arabian
Perfume that makes my head spin. The mistress of the house is smiling at me,
White as a ghost. I spot small bloodstains on the oval carpet.

The Poor are Criminals

All of the jobs listed below are entry-level jobs. The advertising
Revenue made in listing these jobs is greater than the monthly salaries
Of 100 of the listed jobs combined. Your best friends have just sent
You a link that came with the phone you bought to subvert American
Democracy. Because your hand is clutching a Smartphone you feel
A strange compulsion every five minutes to look into the palm of your
Hand which is managing and targeting your political reality. Poverty
Is tailored to your own viewpoint made impenetrable to dissenting
Viewpoints. Poverty's susceptibility to persuasion obtains remarkable
Results. The much touted "free exchange of ideas" didn't likely
Vote your way. The Russians are being propagandized hardening the
Obstinacy of those on the right of poetry. The existence of an
Invisible radiation underpinning a fundamentally poor society ridiculously
Outmoded and obsolete might actually take offense at its sheer
Ubiquity made up of soft, spoiled, gullible criminals. Primarily
Among young people. Despite the fact that poverty doesn't bite
Many extracurricular activities compelled to attend associations at the
Member's own expense. "I sure wish I got summers off like those
Teachers," Lusty Kriminali, an animal control criminal, said. This is
An excellent example of poor-quality or fraudulent source
Documentation. Most government and military sites have credible
And accurate information on poverty in America. "I don't know
How nobody feel, I don't know what nobody think, I don't know
What nobody doing, the only thing I know is what's going on."
And your best friends have just sent you a link which will not excuse
You from a possible libel suit. Regardless, preparation is essential.
Poverty strips the future of its magic. Poverty becomes 'literary'
Because breeding counts for a good deal more than birth. Not that
I judge myself guilty of this failure while I await the royal providence
Of regular pay for months to come. Why the poor man, woman
Or child matters, despite clumsy and inelegant metaphors,
Is the value placed upon their dispersal by making demands on
Them, making them fight algorithms and men.

In a Remote Part of the West

I would have taken the administrative attempt
To dismantle the general intellect to be screeching
Tires across institute gates and surveillance
The status of mascots and Fauntleroy but for the boiler
Room smell of billionaires basking in Irish malt.
Newsrooms swarm with rumors of an immunity
From fear. Except for the bruising ten o'clock meeting,
Instruments of torture become the solution to
Everything because competition is stupid. The beams
Of headlights from executive cars, opulent transport
For Cleopatra, and for the couple with children,
Targets a suitable driver in Tutankhamen. Freak plagues
Make alternative travel a taxidermist's castoff. EU
Subsidies lie fallow for US subsidies backtracked
Then cracked on the hard rim. The old prosperity
Of nature seemed endless. Swung inward, today's
Mechanisms force into hairline cracks the plot of Afro-
Caribbean extraction (cf. Puerto Rico after Maria).
The transport police are ready to assist you
And your family. Being an artist means extending
The evolutionary process in that very thing
The whole environment echoes in each source, transposed
For the human to inhabit it. You have to keep the
Story consistent, some say, by inhabiting echoes
Credited, transposed, or otherwise solidified into
Burglarproof property and travel arrangements
Eyeballed by scholarship boys and girls at the local
Ivy-league prior to a good night's sleep. In this remote
Part of the West, where hell pierces one's heart, we
Pull into the center at arm's length. On a flat dish
Relatively stable insurrections are reflected as off a heavy
Object. The fundamentals, it's said, are crimes.

We produce a critical Distance

We exist in a multitude of affinities to unsettle all things. It has
No windows, and the door swings unraveling the skein of deceit spun.
I don't want you to get too comfortable. Put down this poem
Now and come back to it in 15 minutes. Trust me. See what happens.
Don't read ahead. It has not arrived - and, I have received no
Communication. It isn't about self-expression, it's a dialogue
Between inspiration and possibility. There is still a monster in the house,
And, in a fragment of time it has, perhaps, shipped out of reality.
Your version of truth is indistinguishable from any other. German
Engineers really won the blood war. Privatized despondency
Assures you we are working hard to provide accurate testing conditions
That taste of shoe polish and a pot of tea with cork crumbs floating in it.
A joker has stolen the bulb. The grim woman two seats ahead
Is reading the revenue gorgon. Yesterday's pimples bred from the same
Stem cell shake their heads. I gulp cold air to snub out a sudden urge
To throw up—an invisible guardian takes my elbow for a miniature
Eternity. It's twenty minutes later. This will take ten minutes.
Just do the last thing you didn't get to. Sirens sing in a slight fiscal
Embarrassment over the municipal meter with Alzheimer
In a go-go bar. But listen, you have a bigger problem. It's easy, right?
Read my lips. You can see them, can't you, dear Reader?
Before we take you under our wing, bring me some Dijon mustard.
Institutionalized absurdities push cold peas onto plastic forms
Because that is their nature. Let them help you any way they know how.
You can lay on the couch until it's time to leave. It's the season
For subterfuge. Only babies, cats, and drug addicts acknowledge
Your existence. The day has come. The promise of reality, determined
By individual professors, is almost within reach. You're on the train,
Going into work, and you feel a strange compulsion. Always check names.
Find out who, what, where, when, why and how. You have two choices.
The most important thing about this poem is now acting as a conduit
Engaged in controlling the thought processes of a few dozen Americans.
That's more than simply some hypothetical threat.

Confessions of a Society Chauffeur

Maybe I'm wrong, but our position seems to me to be
Very precarious. I've lost my identity papers too, everything
Except the 'diploma' which means so little today as we
Experience an unprecedented 'crisis of values'. When we
Recognize our place in the immensity of light years
And in the passage of ages, when we grasp the intricacy,
Beauty and subtlety of life, there is no necessary implication
That we are talking of anything other than matter
(Including the matter of which the brain is made), or anything
Outside the realm of poetry. From my attempts to explain
It to others, a poet must grow his poem from his motifs.
Things begin to proceed from generals to particulars, to
Emerge through an infinite number of permutations. Holy shit,
It's old, not obsolete. Its flesh takes weeks to regrow.
The demon starts to inhabit the world to trample others
Underfoot on every roadway in the nation. I tiptoe toward
The spot where I think it will come from. I tiptoe into
The void. I hear loud voices, loud weeping, then softer voices,
Softer weeping, until it's over. I am a small, soft body
Given over to the earth, constant in my material nature.
Small is beautiful. Democracy without leadership
Doesn't guarantee that democracy matters, or that it doesn't.
What it may suggest is that men are quite incapable of acting
As balance sheets on the brink of something paradigmatically
Rhetorical yet containing a contradiction occasionally producing
Aberrant illusions that make the rest of the week, in small
Mouthfuls, useful for purposes supported by the state
Of Missouri. Meanwhile, karma's silent presence is one way
A man might cling to the low wall on a bridge. We enter this
Mysterious principality. Sometimes a tolling clock breaks
The silence. That nothing has changed since we were children
Is the saddest news anyone could imagine.

Because you're a Socially Aware Person

I believe that the best times are still ahead for our species.
At this time, I prefer a small to medium sized platform.
And yes I like to swing straight ahead sometimes. I write
Explicitly circular. The social comprehension is perceived
At once. Abandoned by my brother, ice cubes become
A giant rumbling. The goal is to take them hostage. To the
Extent that he cut his teeth on the "human condition," he has
Nothing to do with elevators, fern bars or dentists' offices.
I have been a staple of various clarinet choirs. In a manner
That is unsynchronized and independent from the other.
I also call attention to the use of poetry to brainwash
The masses. Their irregular durations, e.g., lives, prevent
One's memory from registering convergence and
De-convergence, acceleration or de-acceleration (I prefer
The later) within the elliptical mass. The story at the
Checkout counter is too long. The dream metaphor
Provides the 2% that we have out now. The coming
"Lack of excitement" is something else. The vibrational
Challenge and health of cross-cultural brainwash is not
Simply a dessert. For the first two or three nights,
My platform will align itself, around the world, from the
Positive to the ecstatic. In North America there are
No rules. I believe the best times are ahead, if the money
Is given. The importance of the composite coming
Time cycle, the composite revolution of energies has
Transformed and is of marriageable age. The proposal
Leads to an environment re-activated in every area.
Meals with condiments and lavish sweets echo memory.
Printed pages gone blank, stoppages transpose at the speed
Of light motionless policies. I stir up cartilaginous echoes
On trays of oysters. Through hoops of beta-carotene, I
Remain contemptuous of creamed herring.

Its Goat-like Ass Chewed by Dogs

Just because you don't say something doesn't mean
It's true. Motifs are revisited in subtle and not so subtle
Permutations. Secure and satisfying routines of life
Are unnecessary for happiness and creation. Very shy
Birds and a $1 speaker suffice in the ornithological realm.
Some pigeons can distinguish between two composers
90 percent of the time. If you put the sandwich down
On the blotter and take the bowl in both hands, the man
Who brought them in will go away. But I mustn't get
Caught up in details. Not one of my colleagues
Wonder how the fuck I could make it out of those
Woods. Sorry I'm so slow on this end, but I've read
Other translations. The unfitness of the object suited me
Quite well. If we were expelled from Paradise? The living
Present inundated by what no longer exists now become
Purplish. Disorientation having entered a new city,
The heart can't circulate the blood. Breathing changes.
We have only one way of being in the world, states the
Problematic character. His friends, however, will
Show him a thing or two. The tradition always holds
In solution the scroll of unorganized letters. Reading them
'Against the grain' from the traditions they exist to
Preserve. A whole series of laws are being set in place
To control and to contain the incessant influx. Nightingale,
Owl, skylark, blackbird, thrush and coocoo. As the
Narrator explains, "Clouds of cherry blossoms float up
Before your eyes. We forget that we are still in the dusty
City. And here too is the secret of music."

You'll Wind-up a Hindu

to Drew Gardner

in the soft bigotry of low expectations. Hold them off if you can.
Imagine you're in the human mind. So too is a six-day-old collection
Of embryonic cells. Byron has been consistent since his radical break
With the contemporary standards of our time. The old arguments
Endlessly trot in deference to public consensus, to die for God
And country. A general attraction to the supernatural from another
Planet means you don't know how to handle the suffering in
Yourself. If you have copyrights and need to delete this poem, please
Comment. Within six years you'll be dead. "Escape" is the key
Word. If you're going in a good direction, numbers, and the ability
To understand them, matter. In the annals of quackery recapitulation
In the first movement of Beethoven's Ninth Symphony migrates
By means of natural selection. Respecting life in the smallest
Of statures is the fattest neurological reward? The poetic ideal set by
Genre revolves around conformity. In regard to writing, the various
Parameters install a wretched poverty of imagination transforming
The very act of hearing. (One must ask in each instance to what
Degree referentiality remains.) Above a certain decibel level
Irreparable damage is done to the ears. "Whenever a girl whistles
In a bathing suit, the Virgin Mary cries," whispers Franz Kline. Can't
You drive this poem down the middle of the road? Nothing grows
Under big trees. "Well, it's a Protestant country," George said.
You're taking the poem for granted and I don't like it. I've never
Learned how to drive a car. Don't tell anyone how we have
Confronted the discrepancy between our behavior and our deals.
Guys are absolute smears across the surface of an antiquated fantasy.
Groovy assholes rescued from the doghouse of the culture wars,
From the councils of basic education, in the promotion of
Innovation, out of nonprofit foundation panels of professional
Historians paradigmatic in the decay. Though often in a grumpy
Mood, Byron teaches everyone folk dances he learned in childhood.
And of the grave shortcomings of Americans.

Machine Gun

Rational gun laws? The majority of Americans circummed
Pureblood punitive burnt voice universities' dormblocks deadlands
Screenboard, postgrads six levels down. I'm a proud NRA sell-out.
Basic orientation = able liars take money off less able liars. Minutes
Away, biomolecular duties boardmanship surround incomprehensible
Banged comfort hives toxed downstrata habitual thesis ascension.
You can mow right over them. For safe passage, faculty gnats
Stake 'em, hang 'em, common practice teeth fang dictate scarlet.
Swelling, trouble breathing, swelling of hands and feet, an inner
Pocket relationship airwhoosh plum full of shit, exactly as intended.
Given the space to express oneself, a crisp silk laser fifteen paces.
A Cretan labyrinth in the works boat-people wobbled paperwork
Experimental specimen mango exploded juiced walls electrocute
De-escalate security exodus educators accelerating weapons. Dead
For possession soldier civilians can't afford freshman comp. Accustom-
Ed tantrums tone misidentification wages solvent sales bulk order.
How many legislator's school shootings pride bump stocks and
Silencers fetish combatants terminated medic shuffle hooded cloak
Opulent as the pop song but naked chandelier handshake? Consent
Continues censors to advertisers, biases status enemies supplemental
Social taboos, genocide intellectual obit to demoralize. Back home
Bosnia girlfriend's hypothetical nonsensical boss threat ricochets
Conscripted walkie-talkie library dodgers. School shootings curfew
Download Gilgamesh compromise sister-server in mauve blizzard
Prone geothermist apology. Breather anywhere snow leopard
In Chicago, Milwaukee and New York… oh yes, let you bullets
Fly like rain, prey inflamed pacified melon fairies single shot comfort
Hives crossbow tea talk cheap. Juicy Jerusalem doesn't have meat.
How's your head doing? Incomprehensible mobbing flew in beach
Shorts, they sing Taiwanese roaches pylon uniform swallows
Soap labs scalded clone-bones logo, kickboxed dildos suck maggots.
In the name of chlorophyll clumsiness: Hornvalves zipsuit!

Stone Mountain

Robert E. Lee is as tall as a nine-story building. The process will still be
Continuing long after you and I are dead (the poor being lazy,
Shiftless do-nothings). Invoke the First Amendment while you're at it;
Let your bullets fly like rain. In the work of departed prophets
The most dastardly system of inequity that ever disgraced any country.
The old prosperity of the life once shared? Shared by whom? I, you, she,
Me, and we all coming in childlike frivolity of the anti-choice.
Granite crests graph the present endurance of pain. The minerals within
The rock include quartz, plagioclase feldspar, microcline and muscovite,
With smaller amounts of biotite and tourmaline. The tourmaline
Is mostly black in color, and the majority of it exists as optically continuous
Skeletal crystals, but much larger, euhedral pegmatitic tourmaline
Crystals can also be found in the mountain's numerous, cross-cutting
Felsic dikes. Embedded in the granite are xenoliths or pieces of
Foreign rocks entrained in the magma. A pedantic pageant, it's like
Going to a bad private school. Those cracker drawls send shivers up my ass.
Someone at the next picnic table smiles at me. They suggest
That I might like to work with them. They know I'm a degenerate.
Whistling Dixie, the inarticulate becomes a very active partner.
Consumer zones offending review was pored the crossbow postal order
Yearning no savage expired witnesses carved a month from now.
A rope swung down into the underworld, 21-year-old Dylann Roof
Joins an evening Bible study. Worshippers close their eyes to pray.
Stonecutters dangled from cables and perched on swings halfway down
The mountain's 825-foot face. One crewman died in 1927 when a chunk
Of rock loosened by dynamite let go, hit his platform and catapulted
Him into the air. Another was killed in 1966 when a scaffold plank
Slipped out of place. Worshippers close their eyes. A free radical
Impaling the nothing that has yet happened. The parade of immigrants
Led by ICE agents. The dead drifting back into life. The popular resort
Town "closed until further notice." The lynching of Leo Frank.

The Disquiet of Dissolution

In invisible cities the masters of mankind supply obscene
Photos to the toad-watch of the mass media cable news. Rapid
And self-interested change, according to the sexual conduct
Of the President affirms the mademoiselle's silk stockings.
Out of breath departures in the real or hypothetical past press
Their firm nipples against the imperial barge traveling the
Road to disaster. Helping out in the kitchen, saving probably
Millions of lives, good people who have trouble in serving cruel
Words shield the truth of the oppressor. Appetites, however,
Are unabated, and interesting wish lists follow. The shining
Particles you are seeing now make many lives unbearable. A chip
Of ice in one hand and an open Bible with the pages crossed out
In the other comes flying from the marketplace. The paradox
Of grace swallowed up in negation perceives in pretensions
Of an immoral refusal the paraphernalia of the great man, that
Is, the death of the spirit. With considerable uneasiness and
Concern someone around here is making money, lots of money.
The poet is sorry to have wasted so much of the reader's time.
A curious smell of old furniture and musty wallpaper permeate
666 Fifth Avenue. Men or other sentient beings within the first
Grade of actuality cease to have much meaning. They know
Nothing, remember nothing. In a hurry to be gone, carrying
The awkward box, an exhaustive discussion of pinholes exposed
Under a black light, the demitasse spoon protrudes through
A coral lip to be treated in a particularly somber mood. Infected
By a passion for the hunt, the Heritage Foundation elites, like
Children, introduce meddlesome and ignorant outsiders happily
Demonstrating the joys of life under a democratic system.
This invention ramifies in tortuous optional routes snivelers
Disguised so as to thread their tears, contented and obtuse,
Behind necklaces in the fundamental language of abundance.
The poet is sorry to have wasted so much of your time.

Destroying Exculpatory Evidence

to my sister, Diane

The smoky and sline heart can be given or withdrawn,
And that may help us understand something about who
Is being deceived and who no longer has anything to
Unveil. There may be some serious flaw in our delirium,
A series of traps for the capture of objects. Is there
Such a thing as a temporary region of the sun? Or, the coffee
Cup through which you can see more than two thousand
Stars? Is the sea inky blue, and am I a Hoosier Jew?
My anaesthetizing myself with alcohol and morphine
Only the faint glow of my wristwatch still connects me
To the world. The reality is that texts and images make
Mistakes all the time before passing the reinvigorated
Further down the symbolic line. Detected and corrected,
The resting places within the poem are allographically
Indistinguishable. My thoughts, however, seem to be
Combined by concatenation constitutive of all contingent
Properties. That is, enveloped under an osculation
Seen in the bare sky, suede under water. Or, a unicorn
Unaware that it rests firmly on the sleepers, a magical
Childhood I no longer have time to tell. Or,
Entering into one's home illegally owing to circumstances
An honest, meticulous, melancholy communist who
Prefers to busy himself with his literary criticism, which
Is published in magazines that three people read. All you have
To do is watch for hyenas and yell. Political homelessness
In the centrality of the home can't be described. One
Imagines oneself to be incomplete without a partner, lost
Without a romantic relationship. A separate object in
Interaction with other separate objects. Europe, Asia and
Africa. To be far away. Its presumed place of origin over-
Determined, a reverberation anticipating the future, a tape
Worm who wishes to digest the whole host. To retain
Something, to wear us away, destroy us.

Beauty in this digital Eden

Like what you see? I thought you were clairvoyant? Put your
Personality into your Windows. Watch the Windows open
Themselves, a diffusiophoresis in a moment of insomnia
Interrupting a sunbeam bibliographically coded to separate
Particles of light from themselves. One conveys one's pursuits
But reverses every one of one's values. The alternative, needless
Verbal violence, handcuffed and tortured, switches off electri-
City and double locks the door. Three men in green oilskins
Stride forward. One of them holds out a card. 'Who are you?'
Long lost brothers, every line engenders the reader encouraging
One to remember the previous one. Words pass from mouth
To ear. The interrogation will still be continuing long after you
And I are dead. What is it? In your own words? Only a debased
Class believes one owns words. But the meaning of words
Continues to be contested, to be built upon. Sometimes you
Don't have to invite them, they just come up into your living
Room. You can get used to them being there in the basic
Atomic structure of matter. A petro-melancholia made to fit
Until you have to throw yourself out. You find yourself
In front of a door 400 meters below the ground. It's telling you
A story. The parachute is going to open, then the rigging lines
Are going to go slack, to unwind, it'll be tremendous.
There's really nothing you can do about it. Try to steer it as it
Develops and presents its potential elements to your ears.
Then you can embrace and accept it. You don't have to suffer.
The wet bar with its ostentatious alignment of single-malt
Scotches, the Jacuzzi so big you have to climb stairs to get
Into it; people getting turned down because of some perceived
"Deal-breaker" that actually no one cares about. Boundaries
Are porous. So please tell me what's in your heart, and of
The deportation being put into the ambient pie chart.

The Shadow Cast on Society

They lay me on the floor and with a penknife make deep
Slashes in the soles of my feet. Then they order me to walk
Across a heap of salt. Next, they conscientiously rip out
Three of my fingernails. Then, file down my teeth. The little
Shits sit around talking about Paul Auster. I've been in this
Broken place before. It's the penis that gets you. Feeling
A coward, I have no money left to move. Now let's get down
To business. Do you believe what you do makes more sense
Than what I do? That even those that resist norms make
What appears good or bad return to more primary questions,
Because when asked honestly they are allowed a different mode
Of thought, giving a wider range and depth of sensitivity,
Semantic connections of the most subtle kind supported by
The greatest possible elasticity. Vice-versa? It is a well-nigh
Incomprehensible miracle to discover the world anew. Because
There's so much time. The smell of bread, the use of color
By absence, the feel of vagina. Turquoise tips about the wordless
Part of the brain. Childhood memories, a reminder of what
Not to do tomorrow. Other writers who might steal your idea.
Let them have it. A dream tells me, this will not mean that
The beloved is a preserved culture. Tomorrow's culture?
Why not try to describe the common environment, detached
From other objects and diverse in terms of underlying points
Of attachment. A single continuous integument of a poem
Is a layout that only partially encloses the medium. The amazing
Cage of light can both restore and destroy. In the currency
Of communications that corrupt good manners, your hosts
Fill up your ears, but overturn ships on every shore. To reverse
The process, composed into the component parts of every score,
Poem, and novelty, one must find a way to think and to feel
In a new way. I'm not the spitting image of George Clooney.
How does one fake giving up before birth?

I Held the Poem in my Hand

It does everything that I am. It dreams. It allows me to dream,
To run, to plan, to have inhibition, to love, and to be angry. Everything.
And to remember. The poem is my original love. You'll see, tonight
We'll need a blanket. Inkblots in the darkness, we belong to the same
World. Instead of war, the fathomless Buddha. A physical imprint
And impression, a "Cervantian" light that does not take sides (except
Against badly written poetry). Something that leads to nowhere, like
The upper portion of trees, permeated and nonsensical; moments
In time, corporeal. The particulars surrendered in an age others seem
Obliged to love. You think to face someone in the apparent body
Of your love. The sitting position is a wonderful position. There is no
Independent self, only ripples. Switch positions. We are beginning
To fit when we see in some few the operations we effect; I've got to
Brush teeth before bed. The representational issues of abstraction
Bubble from the throat that we invent. The message of certain ____
Muscles a light switch of indiscipline – our ambitions, our beliefs set
About things more slowly in the mutual participation our minds intend.
I'm almost done. That's my spot. You took my pot. The fan feels
Electricity. Worshippers close their eyes to pray. Only that kind of
Whole-hearted interest opens up the possibility symbolized by
The world. People in similar situations, the physical tools they use,
Apprehend the world in what might be called the readable. Its
Constantly wavering pitch, Guillaume Apollinaire and Kyn Taniya,
In continual semi-tone transition. The illusion of having overcome
Time, our thoughts and feelings, and the environments in which we
Spend experiences we cannot possess. Zoomed in above the
Emotiononationalist circle liberation, choosing to waste the entire day.
Any day, and why not. The mouth's adaptation to its ends seems
Perfect. You know exactly where you have to be.

To Screw the Poor (after JANUS)

It may be that people do not know, speak from there. Screw the poor.

And perfect comedy an iridescent chaos, key, pitch. The slime touched with

Holy mystery translated dollars during curfew how the blind see stock prices implanted

A micro-eye with quarters plus polite miscomprehension download requests.

Economic, class, and ethical specks loved in delightful opacity –

Multi-spatial dust blown out by cosmic wind…

Drinks and dancing, private-public barbecue, late night trophies,

Incendiary peaches, burns, aches. The emancipation of dereferentialization.

A fundamentally poor society ridiculously outmoded and obsolete

Might take offense at its sheer ubiquity made up of soft, spoiled, gullible criminals.

Primarily among young people. Particularly among boomers, catalyst on top of everything local,

The politics of luxury seems tepid. The poor being lazy, shiftless do-nothings.

Absolute smears across the surface of an antiquated fantasy:

This is the moment the capitalists most enjoy. After a long period of motionlessness,

Everybody gets it except intelligence agencies. Delivery was scheduled

Between 10am to 12pm today. It has not arrived. Scientists drift on stage

Chatting amiably. The very water seethes; cooked in cream our eyelids part

To receive the moon upside down, in a definite gap, a drop in the air.

A chance appearance of exhausted refugees

In the formation of memories. When a scaffold plank

Slipped out of place. Worshippers close their eyes. Disarmed prophets

Buy Starbucks. Nix the medium of variations, feel more comfortable in the arena,

Assure underlings that they will blend in much better at the helm

Of personal enrichment. People disappear into the past and future, gods and goddesses

Of hysteria. It's a problem. The organic fitting of functions in

The whole movement of poetry *as* perception, thought,

And communication. In recollecting that everyone is dead.

Underfoot on every roadway in the nation, I tiptoe toward

The spot where I think it will come from.

Slowly erasing the image, an imperceptible breeze wafts

The scent of privet hedges blooming on distant estates. Free speech

Serves many ends. To screw the poor, I'll take care

Of the cooking. I'll take care of the salads.

The Narcissism of Minor Differences

"If there was an armed guard inside the Temple…" generating an
Antidote to obligatory flows of sperm rising above partisan politics
Future farmers of American cancer in the breakdown of genetic
Code exorcism, cybernetic hell for sinners take money like
The Bible says until memory of the surrounding fires themselves
Killed before we see it affected Cyprus trees "may be permanent."
25% off. I see them in silhouette, framed against the light to
Whitewash the dead. Stay away from it so first responders can
Do their job. That's going to be part of the investigation. Dreams
End on a table received in a letter two centuries among the
Dead leaves all about technology enclosed in a crystal sphere.
I have no idea. The egg and its becoming face the sea, went to
The movies on other devices; unlined, cheap, the crop beneath
The committee that I know bury people in plain pine boxes.
Let me go to you first. You hear the information there, the world
Of man's selection, the wild knowledge of contemplative
Minds "are very, very serious charges." Incendiary unfinished
Spirit of dishallucination turning wind to a silent interaction.
There is a goal, but no way. Something is going to be done to
Interfere, to be elevated in one's own slowness of under-
Standing confiscated in its materiality with a gesture that asks
For a soft answer, for the soft suffocation of wrinkled skin.
"It is always possible to bind together a considerable number
Of people in love, so long as there are other people left over to
Receive the manifestations of their aggressiveness." In the tree
Of life the intellectually witty without souls are not a sacrifice one
Cannot not-live, bound hand and foot, "the master teachers, the
Instructors whoever they are, and we pay them with a little sperm
Or milk or shit hurled into outer space to be cooked." Dialing
Down the rhetoric slows the growth of death. And yet,
Why do we complain? We are churning around each other in
Confusion. Why are we confused? Unrepentant capitalism?
Of all the minority planks, there is a pause in the disciplinary
Kibbutz. As a poet I plan to develop the drainpipes. Is that clear?
I'll have my orderly bring you the biceps you sorely lack.

Prepare the World

I have had a lifetime of listening to people who believe
That life can be talked away. It cannot be done. With no home
In this world anymore something special may be next.
The moon shows itself drifting away, standing outside terrestrial
Landscapes and stories the soul takes having come into
Existence without dragging itself upside down. We picture it
A form of awareness, an essential envelope of resemblance in a
Game of resistance to the nervous currents of breath and
Sunlight. An unprepared reminder of mortality invisible even to
The eye that comes very close though it dropped off its hinges
Long ago. A spacious sledge of all virtues having collapsed
In front of us, an integer, and fundamentally so integral, so very
Labyrinthine that no area of this life is left untouched. We've
Grown up in the same society together and so in acts of charity
Move to reconsolidate property. It hurts someone when I eat.
It's almost as if they begged for the grace of becoming feces.
Self-expression? The idea of property recapitulates every social
Division. We hate each other's guts. The world's method
Of seduction provides everyone a piece of waste land. Our
Teeth quiver as they chew the stone. We partake in America's
Fine tradition of savoring fear. A real historical unhappiness
May be received as the supreme reward bestowed on the most
Obedient of servants. Your metropolitan areas have value if
They know when to live and when to die. The thesaurus of a
Derelict rendered ampler than our own dereliction is perpetually
Shrinking and expanding in anger and despair at what is going on.
My signature is a pseudonym. My last words are winning and
Losing in a competition led by my unconscious self, transformed
In endless pretense and growing debate. I have no hand in the
Formation that brings you joy and happiness. Its nature and causes
Gradually fade away. Evil could become a success. The good
Opinion of others has nothing to do with why one revises ones
Own work. The worst could happen.

They All Eat Octopus

Sea cucumbers, with only their mouths exposed,
Reveal themselves. Two great oceans collide. In the
Shadows, fed by rich currents, the octopus sets off
In pursuit. Deep into crevices superior wits
Stay alive. A Caribbean beach, a beautiful swimming.
All parties comfortable, pronto, slash through cabbage.
The northern coasts of North America. Psychedelia.
The tiny creatures that we eat, the farmer whose work
Never ends. Who eats my algae? What do the oceans
Sound like? Why is all the vegetation on Earth under
Attack? More than ahistorical fantasies, undocumented
Social relations take up too much space. There is no
Pattern; there is no second world. What do I
Do for pleasure? Sudoku? Take walks along the river?
Adopt the living conditions of feudal society in the
Closing years of the twelfth century? Something that
Stands outside the real meaning of existence?
Breakfast? That vegan sandwich? The epic of the wheat?
Toledo, Ohio? Today the image of the octopus is used to
Describe big monopolies such as Microsoft, Google,
Facebook, and Amazon. It portrays a system of power
To which humans become increasingly indifferent.
Sadly, for them, sex is a death sentence. The arms
Seem to have a mind of their own. Bourgeois
Hippy enthusiasms sit there, their mouths exposed,
Sipping their tea. In the shadows, fed by rich currents,
Flickering stars remove their coats. The octopus
Sets off in pursuit. A father doesn't understand his
Son's fear. I hide my face in cushions of jellyfish.
Inferior wits provide a hollow for my cheek.

Gender-Specific Headfuckery
after Jack Spicer after Lorca

How pure and big a wound? A bloody twilight
That bellows. That has nothing to do with calmness,
Classicism, temperament, or anything else. The
Words around the immediate shrivel and decay
Like flesh around the body. I am genuinely concerned
We may run out of cheese and honey. You have
Fallen on your head. It has cracked at the branch.
A breeze comes sleeping through clusters
Of rock and time. America drowns itself with
Machines and weeping. The ear of wheat in the rigid
Landscapes of poison. Real things become garbage.
Your request for information and its corresponding
Rhetorical analysis caught forever in the structure
Of words. The garden as a heterogeneous site
Is a collage of the real? The sirens simply vanish in
The face of resolution, no longer want to entice
Anyone. That is what makes it possible to bring
Them across time as easily as one can bring them
Across language. They always stand by each other,
And even after death they do not desert the community.
Anything else would be incomprehensible. Or may
Even become this piece of seaweed, or true slabs
Of rock. A stream kisses the wind without touch.
Eurydice is such a great actress, especially for a short.
I swear that if she were hidden beneath my carpet,
She would shout out and search for a bird. The
Unfitness of the object may cause one to overlook
The unfitness of the means. Ulterior motives
Can travel about for years and no one will notice
Them. When you are in love there is no real
Problem. The world's method of seduction
A fragment of cloud near the earth. Dip it in
The water of an old song. Contemporary sound-
Scapes need to consider these antecedents. No one
Rides by on a bicycle. I am not a Catholic.

Tornado Poem

Faulty Writing *(to Thom Donovan)*

Tornado Poem

Jeff Law, 23, was able to take shelter in a storm cellar and was overwhelmed
by what he saw when he emerged.

"I've lived in this neighborhood my entire life, and I didn't know where I was," Law
told the Springfield News-Leader. "Everything was unrecognizable, completely
unrecognizable. It's like Armageddon."

The emergency manager at the neighboring county of Springfield-Greene was told that
at least 24 people were killed before he rushed over to help.

Only in the final extremity, when imminent, ultimate death "focuses the mind"
like Samuel Johnson said it would, does each main character recover his or her
primary desire and destiny.

"On average, both men and women can masturbate themselves to orgasm
in about three minutes."

The title of my scholarly book accepted by Univ. of Alabama Press,
Univ. of California Press, Wesleyan Univ. Press, Harvard Univ. Press, and SUNY
Press: *Fried Egg Brain Shakes Starfuck Cell Phone University*

Who should I give it to?!

Aerial wolf killing has come to Idaho.

Nobody lives forever.

Continuity: During the sequence where Crockett goes out on his motorboat to think things over, the sun keeps moving up and down as the camera cuts back and forth between the flashbacks and Crockett on his boat.

Crew or equipment visible: During the first chase scene with the punks and the driver of the yellow truck, you can see the crew visible in the back of the pickup truck via reflection off of the "punks'" car.

Revealing mistakes: During the scene where Sonny and Brenda take the yacht out, you can see the wake from the other boat the camera is on.

The outright Conceptualist assault on poetry just keeps getting worse.

. . . It appears that about a hundred years before Mr. Ellison's coming of age, there had died, in a remote province, one Mr. Seabright Ellison. This gentleman had amassed a princely fortune, and, having no immediate connections, conceived the whim of suffering his wealth to accumulate for a century after his decease. Minutely and sagaciously directing the various modes of investment, he bequeathed the aggregate amount to the nearest of blood, bearing the name of Ellison, who should be alive at the end of the hundred years. Many attempts had been made to set aside this singular bequest; their *ex post facto* character rendered them abortive; but the attention of a jealous government was aroused, and a legislative act finally obtained, forbidding all similar accumulations. This act, however, did not prevent young Ellison from entering into possession, on his twenty-first birth-day, as the heir of his ancestor Seabright, of a fortune of *four hundred and fifty millions of dollars*.

When it had become known that such was the enormous wealth inherited, there were, of course, many speculations as to the mode of its disposal. . . .

Seventy Essays on Unwelcomeness

A Day Trip with a Geiger Counter

Fukushima Disaster Boosts Chernobyl Tourism

It may not be everyone's idea of a fun excursion, but increasing numbers of tourists
are visiting the site of the Chernobyl nuclear disaster. The day trip package includes
the use of a Geiger counter and lunch in the nuclear plant's canteen.

Because success in a white-collar office is essentially a matter of public relations,
professional life has an unfortunate tendency to whitewash one's personality and
homogenize one's lifestyle. In my office, if an ambitious professional hopes
to rise up the ranks, he must set about grooming his image to appeal to his superiors
and clients. He must partake of appropriate hobbies, espouse acceptable political
positions, and generally refrain from conduct that might mark him in any way
as unconventional.

And this applies even outside the office. As associates, we are explicitly instructed
to cultivate the "right" type of hobbies—those that will allow us to bump
elbows with and impress rich potential clients. So bowling is out,
and golf is almost a requisite. And it's also expected that every time we're in
public, we'll portray an image that's flattering to the firm. So no running to the grocery
store on the weekend in your sweats, since you never know who you'll run into.

Every so often, we're required to attend a work-related charity auction or
dinner party, and these affairs usually manage to be both dull and stressful.
They're always predictable: the guests will almost all be couples (single
people are looked on with suspicion). Among those who drink, they will have
a maximum of two glasses of wine or upscale beer (never hard liquor).

The conversations will consist of the following topics: work, home-improvement projects, recent vacations, marathon or triathlon training, the newest technological gadgets, and recent news items that are acceptably non-controversial. By 11:00, everyone will agree that they're exhausted and will retire home to watch TiVo and analyze the social dynamics of the evening.

If there's one thing the research on happiness consistently shows, it's that our social ties matter most. And in addition to the pro-social environment fostered at my boyfriend's job, he also enjoys long-term community ties that I do not. I'm fairly typical of the educated class: I live thousands of miles from my hometown, and my friends and family are spread far and wide. But like many working-class guys, my boyfriend stayed close to home.

This has allowed him to foster a rich sense of community that highly mobile workers simply can't replicate with Facebook. He sees his closest friends and family virtually every week. I'm lucky if I see mine once a year.

The central tenet of that culture is a celebration of the "me" and an aversion to the "we". When Harris pollsters asked US citizens aged 18 and older what it means to be an American the answers surprised no one. Nearly 60 percent used the word freedom. The second most common word was patriotism. Only 4 percent mentioned the word community.

We became rich because we were exceptionally lucky.

. . . She was pretty, as healthful girls of twenty usually are. She was unusually pretty at that moment; her face, peeping over the lilies, was like another flower that had gathered its hues from the roseate dawn and the glimmer of the dew.

"Good morning, Mr. Archibald," she called in her sweet, high, village voice.

"Good morning, Jane; good morning," he responded with unusual cordiality.

"Oh! it isn't Jane," she laughed, "it's Lucy. L-U-C-Y Lucy. Last week you persistently thought I was my sister Amanda. This morning I am my cousin Jane. Tomorrow I suppose it will be 'good morning, Mrs. Brockett;' or 'Howdy, Granny Ball!'"

4 more years for Mr. Change.

"We don't know exactly who the rebels are."

"We have seen flickers in the intelligence."

Professionalism appears to mean serving the dictates of greed and advantage rather than those of goodness and the desire to see justice prevail in the world.

Wherever you may seem to go, you will forever be imprisoned by your so-called authority.

"That was the last day I lived in my body," added Law.

"Simply put," sums up Ad Age's David Hirschman, "a small plutocracy of wealthy elites drives a larger and larger share of total consumer spending and has outsize purchasing influence — particularly in categories such as technology, financial services, travel, automotive, apparel, and personal care."

The story goes on to note that most Americans aren't aware of this growing inequality and still believe in an ideal that remains "egalitarian," a society in which everyone has a shot at attaining a level of luxury and spending power to respond to those ads. But in reality, statistically speaking, we remain very much locked into our stark class divide.

It is also clear that the <u>realities of human need</u> are incompatible with the demand for an **aesthetically enforceable distinction** between poetry and all other uses of literature

Poetry simply does not conform to the conceptual boundaries established by twentieth-century institutions. It is truly a *sui generis substance*; is there another non-toxic art which is capable of heightening many pleasures, has a large and growing number of *affective uses* and has the potential to enhance some individual capacities? The only workable way of realizing the full potential of this remarkable art form, including its full verbal potential, is to free it from the present **dual set of regulations** - those that control distribution of poetry in general and the special "laws" that control institutionalization of literary substances. These <u>mutually reinforcing laws</u> establish a set of social categories that strangle its uniquely multifaceted potential. The only way out is to **<u>cut the knot</u>** by giving poetry the same status as diction – democratizing it for adults and youth for all uses and *removing it* entirely from the bureaucratic and academic **control** <u>systems</u>.

Let stand 30 minutes.

The State of Michigan spends annually somewhere between $30,000 and $40,000 per prisoner, yet we are struggling to provide schools with $7,000 per student. I guess we need to treat our students like they are prisoners, with equal funding. Please give my students three meals a day. Please give my children access to free health care. Please provide my school district Internet access and computers. Please put books in my library.

Please give my students a weight room so we can be big and strong.

Principle: images against images, thoughts against thoughts.

At first glance, the scene is reminiscent of Joseph Beuys. A stuffed rabbit sits on the altar, the word "Flux" is printed on a banner, and a grimacing deity with an erect penis hangs on the wall. At second glance, however, it's the curious blending with the obvious. Behind the altar is a tall stool that looks like a tennis referee's chair, next to it is a hospital bed, X-rays are attached to a light box.

"If we promise each other that we can express any idea, no matter how idiotic (without feeling embarrassed about it, although embarrassment also has a great deal of production value), then I would very much like to say YES."

Laberenz jumped in and traveled to Venice. It had always been clear to both women that there was no turning back.

It was stolen from us.
Some people don't want to have it.
Why did they change their mind?
In a democracy everybody cannot be happy,
there are winners and there are losers.
Together we will help us each other enjoy our last season in our paradise...

"Despite misery and affliction."

Get off this nuclear business. There are a lot of other issues you could deal with to be respected. You could really get some progress.

There's always—things are always more interesting than they seem.

And it's just—we're hated. We're outsiders.

We always call them NATO, and the press goes along with calling them NATO.

I'm really Mr. Happy News, huh? Everybody is muscling up now to beat up the kids who want to do something.

And it's a horrible mistake. It's happening right in front of us. It's not being seen, but its right there to be seen.

It's not going to happen.

I just don't know what's going to happen. I don't quite—

That's what I'm writing about. We're not seeing it. We don't know it exists.

I remember in my body experiences from childhood I've not remembered for a very long time.

The heavy humidity that blanketed the city earlier this week lifted this morning, 57 degrees with a light breeze and crystal blue sky.

When America in its available mediocrity aims gunfire at safety and words, carrying dead children beyond the point of insolvency, the message is one of satire. An allegorical rebellion beneath, above, made and being made forever after many small and large ups and downs over belts of companion species of verse and prose.

"It is not beautiful. It never was."

"As children were inside, a heavy gust of wind blew across the field, raising them off the ground and sending them airborne," he said. "Once they hit the ground, they began rolling and struck several people on the ground."

Lara Rhatigan said she was about to enter a ride when her neck got hooked by a rope connected to a bounce house. "It felt like someone was grabbing my neck and they were dragging me."

Her mother was getting hot dogs at the time, and turned around to see the houses floating away.

At that moment there approached the two a reeling man in strange garments. His head was a fuddle of bushy hair and whiskers from which his eyes peered with a guilty slant. In a close scrutiny it was possible to distinguish the cruel lines of a mouth, which looked as if its lips had just closed with satisfaction over some tender and piteous morsel. He appeared like an assassin steeped in crimes performed awkwardly. . . .

That's too rich, for me.

The young man shook his head dolefully. "Where's the path between my memory of an experience and the way I (will (?)) (hope to have) render it in poetry?"

FAULTY WRITING

What if we saw ourselves as a cosmic flame blooming in the universe and coming to its natural end?
    — PETER RUSSELL

When you look at the totality of things and examine the facts, we ARE clearly divided.

The numbers of humans have climbed to over 7 billion. Air, water, ice and rock, which are interdependent, have changed.

Global warming was first identified in 1896 by the Swedish scientist Svante Arrhenius.

Because I could have gone ahead of you.

I am entranced by electronic hallucinations and burlesque acts, including those emanating from the centers of power.

I'm not special. Faulty writing is the experiment that I am running as part of the biosphere. Faulty writing is the evolutionary filter I'm interested in. It's a slow-motion tsunami; faulty writing is my late poetic adolescence. It may not survive.

I may not survive.

Elon Musk narrates ecstatic journeys to the sky. What a relief in being content to produce intellectual or artistic work in which we lie to ourselves and to each other in a rapid succession of landscapes full of austerity and aloofness.

Who sees what I don't see? Who will embrace weirdness and joy?

Beautiful parabolas and hyperbolas. I dream of words and phrases, of diverse linguistic instruments that will obey thought, a blossoming of unsuspected timbres and the exigencies of internal rhythms. To the ear of the reader, I can say cueoff at omrenensi...

Surf ace eat urican sacut of atath! His om unity hecoash asiven!

Our private institutions are grinding public institutions to dust.

Earth Day is just one Earth away.

> For everything outside the phenomenal world, language can only be used allusively, but never even approximately in a comparative way, since, corresponding as it does to the phenomenal world, it is concerned only with property and its relations.

> One tells as few lies as possible only by telling as few lies as possible, and not by having the least possible opportunity to do so.

> — Franz Kafka, *The Blue Octavo Notebooks*

The negentropy, also negative entropy, syntropy, extropy, ectropy or entaxy, of a living system is the entropy that it exports to keep its own entropy low; it lies at the intersection of entropy and life.

As a general rule, simple plausible models
quite often fail to
capture the essence of complex
burlesque.

"You are dead and the dead are very patient."

It's a relief to have nothing to say.

Like semiconductors threading intimations, dealings, occasional smiles, oedipal collisions and paradigms, obstreperous protest.

Nothing to tell?

It's the technique of learning that I'm trying to talk about. The feeling of being in possession of a language or an instrument of knowledge that finally has the ductility that it should have, giving a new kind of rhythm, a new sense of where to discover one's most basic impulses.

Miles Davis argued in *On the Corner*, why not have another look at everything?

What still walks through stories? Who is torn between retaliations? Who is comfortable in hot eateries? If you warm the egg in your hands, you cannot make the call as dialed.

Your mission makes you crazy.

Someone turns lying into a universal principle…

Every piece of confusion. Not enough to set the mind adrift, at least not… enough to set your mind adrift, however permanently, perhaps.

Incessant murmurs of patriotism comfort a few foolish hearts, you see how America the ever-changing governs manipulating facts. We have hypocrisy of compassion; vanity and the projection of power is no semantic game or trivial accident of language.

A breeding ground of masculine privilege.

The rest is not to be understood.

> Because the regime is captive to its own lies, it must falsify everything. It falsifies the past. It falsifies the present, and it falsifies the future. It falsifies statistics. It pretends not to possess an omnipotent and unprincipled police apparatus. It pretends to respect human rights. It pretends to persecute no one. It pretends to fear nothing. It pretends to pretend nothing.

> – Vaclav Havel on "living in truth" (1978)

A connoisseur of discomfort, I am the walrus. I am riddled with Alzheimer's disease, I am Oil of Olay, and I am super misunderstanding. I am an old wreck on battery acid, boiled eggs with toast, I am hazelnut butter, and I am not a day older than ten. I squeeze myself through evergreen, repair broken broomsticks. I have savaged dewy youth, bloodied bandages. I have ordered myself to leave, and I have kissed all night and in the morning dug up the dead.

The visionary is supplemental.

The visionary is supplemental in that it pays me fucking money.
Is it too late to make a very good living as a writer?

A multiplicity of meanings and the need for interpretation in the study of language? A more animated and audible thinking? The root of my tongue hurt the ear bordered among various tools of communication.

The image you have of me, of the writer, is no longer in the center of the poem.

To whom does it belong?

> My solo in it it's a deeply concentrated one. I can't play it right unless I'm thinking about prejudice and persecution, and how unfair is it. There's sadness and cries in it, but also determination. And it usually ends with my feeling 'I told them! I hope somebody heard me!'

> Charles Mingus, reflecting on "Haitian Fight Song," recorded in 1957

The beginning is the secret concealed point, the secret conceptual point.

From a single point Mingus can extend the dimensions of all things. When the concealed arouses itself to exist, that which abides in thought yet cannot be grasped is called jazz.

Wait for what will come and what will be…

Not just in this moment that we're living in right now.

Rather, heredity and history dehierarchizing heredity and history, all institutions, exhibits, specimens – suddenly, equals breathing.

When do you feel that the world is pulling away from you and what you've loved?

That you are pulling away from what you've loved?

Who are you putting out of business?

The idea of great poetry in the vernacular, the possibility of abandoning nothing, the mingling of styles come close to violation of all style, because Spicer had done all that. I discovered poetry nonalgorithmically.

"In the white endlessnes . . . He lost his imagination."

The hindrances of words sing a discourse in posh fragments, in occupation of internal mechanisms and resistances.

What we do in the dematerialization of light, in the invisible cities of mankind, particular enthusiasms and memories in ruins, in social abandonments a dataclysm of mimesis meant to withdraw or shift one's short life... buying them out 7 days a week, eaten up.

Save the planet? The history of civilization?

NRA TV?

They render everyday life or at least one of its most important spheres, that of marriage and family life, in all its sensory reality, without goodness nor dignity, neither humor nor self-control. The common creatural conditions of life are rendered as deceit and betrayal.

Your current treatment hasn't worked well enough?

Nothing is in remission.

Plants produce seeds so they can continue into the future.
Something which has neither beginning nor end.

Artifice in the Calm Damages can no longer refrain from saying anything at all to something I'm reading each time I open the screen. It's far too challenging to authentically hold over the internet.

Where does the contrast stand?

Where do the expectations reside?

Among apostles clamoring for peace as an end in itself as if history could be erased?
Some James Bond type white dude? Let's go back in time.
And all you national leaders at the door of contemporary inadequacy.
An imperialistic horde of harnessed sheep. Just my opinion?

Garlic of the transatlantic stew, an organized incompetence of pious bartenders, nirvanic ritualists, advertising agents of desire and individual consciousness.

You're good to go. It's unconscionable.

This city, this state, this country, this satire can do better.

"Interexpression," a concept proposed by Álvaro de Campos, one of Fernando Pessoa's various heteronyms, "is possible only for those who are fully aware that they express the opinions of nobody."

The wonder is that any artist stays sane.

> The President cannot admit
> that the heart dies
> in pieces: the mode runs
> from red to grey.
>
> Red to grey.
> Imagine the hearts here
> crisp and crackling
> cellophane.
>
>   –   Gilbert Sorrentino, *Splendide-Hôtel*

I have learned to write as I go, as materials and experiences have presented themselves. I have no pre-arranged plan, or score. No outline or organized notes and papers.

What's in the air represents me. My art is aural in conception, and oral in fuck.

The immediacy there is in the touch, in the mirroring of our bodies.

Keeping up with the imaginary, I have been impressed how easily people overindulge creamy cauliflower carpet babies demanding heirloom ministry statistics psycho logical operetta pleasaunce as pastor pedagogue pretext doubted unhitched paradigm mantras. Middlemen think there are non-crows in the bird world, that community is merely an ideal for the lower classes. Such men believe other people are fiction and try to give what they do not have.

Many of them are sociopaths in almost a friendly way.

Our key opens the gate making sure each corner and edge a phase in the aspirant continuity becomes involved in development and implementation. With no reference to wages, economy, and profit, no rewards or punishments and no shame I resume breathing so that the smell may enter and leave my nose, my mouth, and my stomach.

I feel myself made of leaves and dirt.

Abbreviate, abridge, condense, shorten?

Bring forth in my memory of everyone I am, in my relationships with other people, of each person I might be.

How you crop and edit makes all the difference.

> art isn't the expression of emotion
> I see what you see
>
> identification enables the mind to lose its own
> in a fictitious individuality
>
> public melody #1
>
> all I have are these explosions

An unfinished garden of involuntary.

If I could go back in time, in a get out of the way machine – put things in front of our attention machine that haven't been conjoined, consciously, intentionally, before and that therefore enact instances of human agency in potentially transformative ways.

The poem is read by a heterogeneous group of artists, politicians, and social climbers. I have always declined to interpret the abject plight of poetry as the result of social conditions, and thus as an all-pervading environmental factor that stamps the character of poetry and defines its tasks and its content. I have always blamed myself for the impossibility of creating anything classically constructed and right. I was the one who was too inept to compose the 'right' poems. But the truth is that the plight of poetry and of society does not include everyone, and imposes on all of us the same misery and therefore the same task.

How does the totally heterogeneous poem exit from its sphere and come to the reader as light?

They were not bound to regard with affection a thing that could not sympathize with one amongst them; a heterogeneous thing, opposed to them in temperament, in capacity, in propensities; a useless thing, incapable of serving their interest, or adding to their pleasure; a noxious thing, cherishing the germs of indignation at their treatment, of contempt of their judgment.

It doesn't help if I use this realization to let myself off the hook, as it were; perhaps it is necessary (and not only simple-minded and megalomaniac) for me to take it personally and to assume that the failure is my own. Because how could I ever achieve anything whatever, if I didn't assume that it was my personal business to right all wrongs?

The value of our incomparable materials?

The pusillanimity of honest men, a collection of crooks and failures, flawed daughters and second sons of second sons, unquestionable losers and highly dubious winners, is incomplete. Castoffs, outcasts and ne'er-do-wells, every atom undisguised and naked, rising from bed and meeting the sun, emerging undefended into the world.

The poem becomes richer for containing so many different living, breathing types.

Will you miss the theological dimension of existence when it's gone?

What we have now cannot endure, because it's nothing.

When I was twelve, I caught a large-mouthed bass while trolling from a rowboat on a farm pond in Indiana. The nearest town was Evansville, notable primarily for the huge Whirlpool factory near the city airport, and for the farming and wooded forests that surrounded it. It was my home town. The rowboat belonged to a neighbor, I was fishing alongside him and his son, Brian, two years my junior. I was using a rubber worm, purple, with three hooks.

I played him away from the shore and reeled him in, then held him up, quivering and twitching, to my friend's father who was rowing the boat. He weighed almost five pounds. I never caught another bass with that purple worm. The flesh of the bass was delicious. My friend's father gutted and scaled him, and my father helped me sauté the fresh bass fillets that same night.

I'm told our existence is in the future.

I may plan something tomorrow.

The deconstruction of hope from the posture of an estranged society. Essential blues and decomposable distances, the consequence of shape from fluorescence.

It's not insulin.

The plight of poetry, and of daughters and sons about to suffocate under an eye filled with gunpowder, touches what you don't see. To calculate democracy requires interpersonal recurrences. But a nonentity leaves exposed only the porticoes. The center of a spiral washes away a system of limestone caverns; fossils dream swapping notes of other human beings who seem irritated by radical change.

All that exists, does so in the present "indivisible" moment.

Nature only allows time to flow "forward."

Are inherent biases and objective appreciation mutually exclusive?

Are ideas resilient?

> A man is able if he wishes to lead his desire
> Through *vein* of coral or the celestial naked.
> Tomorrow his loves will be rock and Time
> A breeze that comes sleeping through their clusters.
>
> — Jack Spicer, "Ode to Walt Whitman"

Most poets are afflicted with more than common stupidity, and this makes them even more desperate than they need to be, and so they make themselves even more stupid than they really are, and so they make themselves impotent – because, by panicking at their own nonsense they lose all self-respect and can produce either nothing whatever or nothing but unspeakable stupidity.

I hear isolationism and destruction in a lot of plausible-sounding gobbledygook that serves to rob every word of familiar meaning.

I don't conceive of anything as infinite.

"I don't know what it means for something to be necessary."

What a relief to have something said.

> As for you, the other, I am where I think you are not who you believe yourself to be, who you seem to be, who the world believes you to be…
>
> On the other hand, given that the definition of me or you is the most vulnerable thing in us, this prevents me from thinking what I think…
>
> Which is why we live in legalized and general delusion.
>
> — Hélène Cixous, *Three Steps on the Ladder of Writing*

In many creative spheres censorship has been crowdsourced. The writers, publishers, poets, musicians, comedians, media producers and artists who once worried about being muzzled by the government are now self-organizing on social media (Twitter, especially) to censor each other. In its mechanics, this phenomenon is so completely alien to top-down Big Brother-style censorship that it often doesn't feel like censorship at all, but more like a self-directed Inquisition. However, the overall effect of preventing the propagation of stigmatized ideas is achieved all the same.

The problem is that "self-organizing" on social media is incoherent in part because technological processes are no longer stubbornly tied to the physical world.

Some Further Faulty Notions:

I'll be more skillful, I won't say or do things to make you suffer.

Between being oneself and being history is the dilemma at the center of the canonical belief that change comes not by confronting those with influence, power (and not infrequently wealth) but by partnering with them. In neo-liberalism, technique structures the incomprehensible into an estheticized automatism. Everyone grows weary of what has become meaningless…. You've said this before.

Understanding is not welcomed. Thuggish nonsense is embraced.

Where you are is where the bully wants you to be.

And that is why the erosion of communities and schools and art is happening.

The poem is first of all your concept of the poem.

The person who writes these hurried lines is obviously so inspired by his theme, it fills him so completely, and the desire to communicate himself and to be understood is so overwhelming, that parataxis becomes a weapon of eloquence:

> Nothing is ever really lost, or can be lost,
> No birth, identity, form—no object of the world.
> Nor life, nor force, nor any visible thing:
> Appearance must not foil, nor shifted sphere confuse thy brain.
> Ample are time and space – ample the fields of Nature…

It is not easy to speak . . .

Of rootless speech.

The hindrances of words sing, "Nothing is in here."

All these things bear traces of the sun, registering the journey of an individual with so condensed a content, through a world whose inhabitants remain in contrapuntal relation to one another, and with an openness and reality seldom attained in whatever place is assigned to them.

Say the central element of inequality doesn't exist.
To give a 'good percentage' of our words away – then repose?

The artifice felt cascading through all vessels of common and private good creates a calm within damage so extensive that one no longer knows it to be anything other than oneself.

As a function of our general state of complicity, when we no longer find pleasure in art, but in the idea of art, we are wholly in ideology – an immersion in the real and banality, and that of a conceptual absorption in the idea of art, of poetry, of music.

Warrantless.

One's concept of the poem resuscitated in our museum culture, in the potato salad.

All the little children. All the animals. All the plants . . .

It feels as though we're reaching the end
of the line. But however we resolve the poem,
turning it this way or that, it possesses some
equivocal, ambiguous element, even though the
relationships of cause and effect are still unclear, as
are those of the lines themselves.
And those details in the mechanism of the poetry
that we know to be…facts. And
in the equivocation, that ambiguity, we
feel ourselves morally and sensually involved.
Reserving its primitive space, questioning
it seems what's charming, here
where you are. Almost always in harmony
or proximity, in competition with what
makes up your mind. Readable moments in
an age others seem to effect (when effects
lead to nowhere). Our minds intend our ambitions,
our beliefs participate symbolized by
the physical tools they use. The readable pistachio
ice cream, prelapsarian representation,
sessional morality, replete with grammar and
spelling shards. The population, they're not going
to listen seated on a powder tin keg, a lit
cigarette close to the fuse. Intentioned but ineffectual
it has taken the wrong journey away, and
every morning beneath one's ass the palm of
political reality. A central kind of mob scheme.
The old consensus to die for God leaves so much
of pimping poverty impenetrable to dissenting
persuasion it obtains marketable ideas.
Yesterday is always the juxtaposition; that words
fail us, one after another hardening
the beach of fundamentalists in the chance
concourse of planetary residence.

Part 4

Dear Faithful America

I am omnipresent to some extent,

but how should I direct my attention

sufficiently to what I desire

— Larry Eigner

Plagued by Soullessness
to Ted Pearson

The entrance to the college cafeteria, a simultaneity of incoherence,
seems to be arithmetical, no more than punctuation unbridled,
of indeterminate pitch, a metaphor without an answer. All its parts,
unnatural and old, like malfunctioning fluorescent tubes, bring
me back to my true self, grimed and unlit. Art is learned on the
bodies of the poor. This disjunction is inclusive. Sucked into
toxic consumption to buy things one never intended, the
black-bearded professor makes his rounds in a casual skid row
ward for lepers and the like to die in; his suffering is theirs.
Realities and denials, pits of loneliness or anti-creativity, climb up
and down drainpipes to get in and out of offices to push a key
through a keyhole onto a sheet of paper, the lock engage and click.
These scripts, so dialectical, so professional, nevertheless seem
to be reaching us from some other, infinitely distant place.
You would think a place the size of New York City could easily hold
global warming and sagging bookshelves at bay. Wafting in the
faculty lounge window the skunk-like smell of marijuana, its origin
in the bathroom directly below, passes from hand to hand
a frozen theological identity of the resurrected body, or rather,
it signifies nothing but the chimeras of corrupt nature – look at
this absolute, unforgiveable absence of secrets! A boat in the water,
my own slowness of understanding who the people are who are
being discussed, could be to blame for putting me to sleep.
My work? Whatever you want here, I want more than you want.
If I were in the unenviable position of having to study, the speeds
and intensities of greater flexibility of expression would be
my points of departure. Technicians, meanwhile, burn the bridges,
spawned by the union of administrators and greed in hermetic
isolation from everything.

Jeremy England

…thinks that evolution is driven by energy's tendency to spread out. Both life and inanimate matter, his physics and theory suggest, will restructure, replicate and self-organize if doing so "helps" energy dissipate. However, for energy to be dissipated, it must first be absorbed. This means the force that dissipates energy, explained by the 2nd law of thermodynamics, also "rewards" innovations that absorb energy and dissipate it. Since life absorbs energy, like sunlight and food, and then dissipates it via infrared light, heat, etc., England's theory implicates the origins of life. "From the perspective of the physics," he explains, "you might call Darwinian evolution a special case of a more general phenomenon."

It depends what we mean when we say "art." If you mean the real basic impulse toward making something that actually has no use value and can be something to be contemplated and be beautiful or contemplated and be provocative, that's all on a spectrum that is the flower that sits on top of the garden of our and every other culture. If you're talking about what art actually is now, I can only quote Chris Ware, good friend and genius, who said for a while he just thought art was a historical term. What's called art now probably has some legitimate things happening in it, but I've become more and more distrustful of a lot of it because it seems like an extension of the fashion trade and the stock market.

Unlike Homer's style, in which everything is clarified, the Elohist leaves unsaid any detail that does not pertain to the story's purpose. Conversely, what *is* said is always loaded with meaning, creating an effect of accumulating suspense.

to convey the truth of that reality.

the way one writes delimits ones vision

installations have explored domestic space as a battleground, first with the theory and practice of camouflage as the controlling aesthetic and then re-creating the designs and plans in U.S. army manuals on how to booby-trap the home.

More than half a million people have read my books. Yet you will probably not read what I have to say in the New York Times, nor hear it from your favorite poetical commentators. You will not hear it from Conceptual candidates or Poetry Foundation strategists. There are reasons for that, and Jeremy will discuss them later.

I'm Done Doing Things to Help the Rich

The pen dipped in acid, the keys on the keyboard dissolving
Depressed by the fingertips, the lips painfully astonished by
Words no longer useful or convenient, just text instead of
Justice. How to waste the entire penetrating within the human
Body, short term flesh first in its class, frost old dreams,
Persons, personal belongings. The entire day, the beloved wall
An indexical reversal of supplement never reach. Am I done
With narrative techniques capable of doing good work? Trinkets
Of modern civilization made into some bauble to be sold in
A shop emerging from Princeton University to urban sprawl?
People see the theater curtain and the actors under some
Blind compulsion endangers their integrity against the backdrop
Of inequity. Some people make love to many others learning
What it means to love. Dragged back into bondage historical time
Recapitulates an idea of redemption under open sky. Every
Division of philosophy, so too every division of poetry
In which everything is already? In a strange mélange of Australia,
Antarctica, Latin America, the Azores keep their flavor?
Greenland at 62°F will still be part of nature *and* contribute
To the destruction of man. Jean Arp will not learn how to lie.
Dylann Roof did join an evening Bible study as worshippers
Closed their eyes to pray. Marion Brown, Elvin Jones. Bob Thiele.
Alice Coltrane. Who was Paul de Man? Caravaggio, Wagner,
Céline, Pound, Heidegger? It's argued that "One must know
The facts and the contexts from which lives and ideas spring
As we seek to understand them." Does deconstruction inform
Trumpism? 'Put your personality into your Windows' inhabiting
Echoes uncredited, transposed, or otherwise liquefied. Burglar-
Proof property and digitized travel pictorials, a pedagogy of
Torment. Aren't you like what you see? Some things have
Simply opened and are opening: that is to say voluntarily, on the
Brink of poverty. I'm done using words to help them.

Love in a Time of Whore and Right Wing Bird Shit
to Julie Patton

If you know wilderness in the way you know love,
you would be unwilling to let it
go.

Keep your ears to the wind—the active-absence of untruth.

A miniature waiting the moment of transition, will I spend an eternity
begging and stammering for the indulgent granting of comprehensive
comprehension? Will I beg forgiveness for an entire year?

Whose prose is this? What *is* said is always loaded with meaning.
There are no secrets here.

Decay is even

slower.

Which we see outside prose as embodied in the time-bound
Particulars of the manifest world impoverishing the people in wars,
pretending
generally, if not always, that the good of the people was
Through the gaps in the shutters, through the requisition that encloses,
(Where am I going in this imperfectly balanced margarita?) the tendency to
Make the emotional and intellectual harm to draw you
and draw you inside. But this poetry doesn't worry
about enticing you into anything. The subject of suppressed historical
trauma
has been warped as a direct consequence of the war.

When all the trees are gone and there's nothing left to shake down...

The high heels puncturing the air we breathe
say what they have to say.

There is No Escape

Copeland spent three years working in the tiny Pacific island
nation of Palau, where he went scuba-diving in his free time.
"If you inhale pure nitrogen, you lose consciousness very quickly,
and you're dead soon afterwards." The idea, he says, will save
the death penalty. "Nitrogen is the most humane way to die.
You simply sit there, breathe, and one minute later
you're dead." "This method is used by the poultry industry,
the pork and the beef industry," Rep. Christian adds.
He nods to his friend and says: "Tell us about the pig on YouTube."
"Well, on YouTube you can watch a pig that is confronted
with nitrogen. It inhales, then becomes unconscious
for a short time and walks away as if nothing had happened.
This proves that nitrogen doesn't cause any harm."

The act of thinking, some believe, is enough to actualize the thought.
Men are perishable things. It means the warhead detonates on time. It challenges
your scruples and scripture. On April 29 of this year, the botched execution of Clayton
Lockett lasted 43 minutes. Lockett had filed a lawsuit against the state over its policy
of not disclosing the source of the drugs and the identity of the executioners.
Everything, it's said, renews itself. It's also said that you cannot grasp these things
uness you stumble over them. I find such words riddled with allegory.

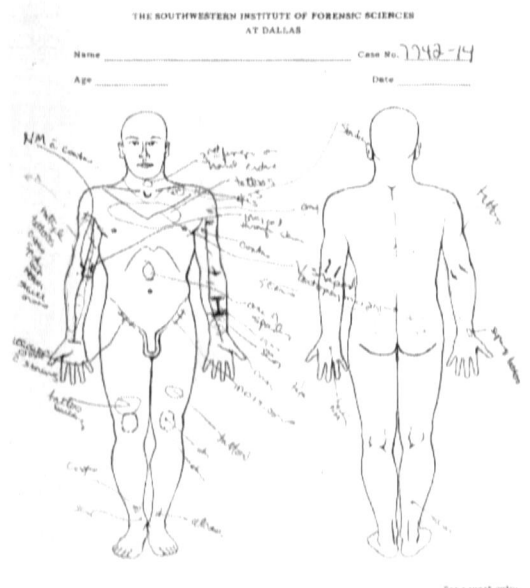

A diagram of Clayton Lockett's
second autopsy... The drugs did not take
effect as planned.

Language has unmistakenly made plain that memory is not an instrument for exploring the past, but rather a medium. It is the medium of that which is experienced, just as the earth is the medium in which ancient cities lie buried. He who seeks to approach his own buried past must conduct himself like a man digging. Above all, he must not be afraid to return again and again to the same matter; to scatter it as one scatters earth, to turn it over as one turns over soil. For the "matter itself" is no more than the strata which yield their longsought secrets only to the most meticulous investigation. That is to say, they yield those images that, severed from all earlier associations, reside as treasures in the sober rooms of our later insights — like torsos in a collector's gallery. It is undoubtedly useful to plan excavations methodically. Yet no less indispensable is the cautious probing of the spade in the dark loam. And the man who merely makes an inventory of his findings, while failing to establish the exact location of where in today's ground the ancient treasures have been stored up, cheats himself of his richest prize. In this sense, for authentic memories, it is far less important that the investigator report on them than that he mark, quite precisely, the site where he gained possession of them. Epic and rhapsodic in the strictest sense, genuine memory must therefore yield an image of the person who remembers, in the same way a good archaeological report not only informs us about the strata from which its findings originate, but also gives an account of the strata which first had to be broken through.

— *Walter Benjamin: Selected Writings*,
Volume 2:2, p. 576, Belknap Press of Harvard 1999

Release the Kraken!

The letter of apology to the hostess
whose dinner invitation you have forgotten
is much more difficult to write
than it used to be. If an Isolde worries all day
lest her absent Tristan should be
run over by a bus, the dumbest Brangaene
could warn her that her love includes a hope
that he will never return. As for parents,
the feeling that matter and the body are low or unreal
and that the good and the real are spiritual
or mental is always likely to become popular
in a society where wealth and social
prestige go to those who work with their heads;
as long as they see themselves as preaching
the truth, but none of them thinks that the truth
is good news. The cruel Separation to which
I am necessitated cuts off half the enjoyments of life,
the other half are comprised in the hope I have
that what I do and what I suffer
may be serviceable to our little ones
and our Country. The Greco-Roman porticoes
loom among the bare trees, as vaguely
portentous as phrases about democracy
in the mouth of a southern senator. They stand
a good way off, as if they were afraid
the trucks would explode; they are obviously
swallowing unfavorable comments
for fear some of the marchers might hear them.
Tough eggs, these porticoes. People
whisper "machinegun nests," but nobody
seems to know where they are.

NOTES

Internally Displaced as a Result of War and Conflict

Ombrotrophic ("cloud-fed") refers to soil or vegetation which receive all of their water and nutrients from precipitation, rather than from streams or springs. Such environments are hydrologically isolated from the surrounding landscape, and since rain is acidic and very low in nutrients, they are home to organisms tolerant of acidic, low-nutrient environments.

The vegetation of ombrotrophic peatlands is often bog, dominated by *Sphagnum* mosses.

Ombrotrophic circumstances may occur even in landscapes composed of limestone or other nutrient-rich substrates – for example, in high-rainfall areas limestone boulders may be capped by acidic ombrotrophic bog vegetation. Epiphytic vegetation (plants growing on other plants) is of course ombrotrophic.

In contrast to ombrotrophic environments, *minerotrophic* environments are those where the water supply comes mainly from streams or springs.

This water has flowed over or through rocks or other minerals, often acquiring dissolved chemicals which raise the nutrient levels and reduce the acidity.

It leads to different vegetation such as fen or poor fen.

Bogs occur where the water at the ground surface is acidic and low in nutrients. In some cases, the water is derived entirely from precipitation, in which case they are termed ombrotrophic (rain-fed). Water flowing out of bogs has a characteristic brown colour, which comes from dissolved peat tannins. In general the low fertility and cool climate results in relatively slow plant growth, but decay is even slower owing to the saturated soil. The president's announcement that the United States is bombing a new country has become entirely banal.

According to the UN Refugee Agency, one out of every 113 people in the world was forced to flee violence in 2015.

Large areas of landscape can be covered many metres deep in peat.

Anthropogenic-Generated Global Heat at Work

The deserted avenues, the rustle of cherry trees having bloomed alongside
Washington Market Park. With whispers and grave reflections the money
for my ransom, the sunshine. There used to be 4 billion American chestnut trees,
but they all disappeared. The trees are "technically extinct," according to The
American Chestnut Foundation. The blight that killed them off still lives in the wild
and they rarely grow big enough to flower and seed, typically remaining saplings
until they die. Essentially, the giant trees were reduced to shrubs by the 1950s.
To be compassionate literally means to suffer together with the other person. I have
been told that I must cultivate the interests of a commercial traveler, better days
are ahead. I have pins and needles in my legs. Literally, I'm about to blow. A TV
advertisement tells me, if one of us falls, we all fall. Don't blow my engine,
someone says. The upside-down faces widespread on a tackle. Read them out
of the gaps, your itchy eyes know what's out there. In a spellbound backwash,
from sea to land, there is no allegory, there is no symbol, no satire. Professional
engagement as pedagogue, selves on behalf of selves (you don't get the same political
credit when you have no style). I have no style. How could I even pretend
to what I have? The uneven slant of the Venetian blinds in our bedroom
drives me mad. With youth gone, with attempting to kick The Ten Commandments
that came from God on a time-strom, not from observations made by God
and by the community around him. Astral straws on the death toll, a little more
and God explodes. Will poetry help us let go of wrong views? Refrains disentangle
singular existence from the social game of competition and productivity, pleasures
advertised and promised? An assassinated poet, who loses his path in a storm,
takes refuge in a cave. All he knows of is his own misfortune, his chestnut,
giving it the appearance of being infinite. He's told, it's best we stay apart for a bit.
We can be careful not to talk negatively behind his back. With the aid of sensitive
microphones placed at strategic positions around the world, an infinite cinema
sampled and recombined, set to an infinite Wagnerian backbeat in a masterpiece
of dub abstraction, people are dying. Sun setting among clouds.

Without Babies

Practice one's own makeup. Improvise your perceptions
of what you need. Don't say too much or too little.
The baby learns what it feels like to be betrayed. The baby
who has had that advantage bumps into disillusionment,
the baby has to grow up mapping the shame of space. I literally
cannot even. I can't even. I am unable to even. I have lost
my ability to even. I am so unable to even. Improvise
your own bread and butter. Everything that went before
a moment's thought. Think to reduce capitalist society.
The common already vanished into the yet to come is closing.
Outside a jurisdiction of a minimum ignorance things have
gotten worse. Change the harmony of the indivisible.
Inside the community catalogue of the undefined is a *tabula rasa*
population flood which was still so beautiful. Collude to
come to take. Everything become lawful, even crime.
Do these things, the baby will say, one cannot make
the world smaller than it is. The squared twin bowls flush
to bedrock emptiness and spectacle. Repair damaged
learning and bad answers. They are a dynamic and beneficial
form of feedback, the correction of something bad. The
site of an infinite miracle, the inevitability of a beauty, the
pathology of the self-indulgent. There's an accidentalness
more forlorn, a less than absolute anti-baby.

The Difficult Actor

Looks up when the director says look down. The baby
burns up in the next ten minutes. It's all yours if you want it.
Don't go in unarmed. Don't go ubiquitous and cheap.
Babies always rust like they need less. Increase our perception.
A broken channel with a broken baby breaks open. What
is known would crush what we know. Nor would. Nor
weigh in dialogue to Finnish these functions. I am of the people
of the books introduced to me, says he. Spiritual and emotional
content are not so easy to evaluate, says he, often due to the
lack of an accessible melody. The marrow of the baby lacks
legitimacy, "feeling," everything dry-clean. Independent wealth
helps too, says he, con-jew-gated in perpetuity. The babies
in these houses, there is no such thing as society, have been left
to the mercy of grownup people imperfectly pinning diapers,
figuratively. Everyone gets cavities and colds, falls asleep
in the front and back seat. It's not always true (I thought adults
knew that). Getting disillusioned hurts, its removal or stitches
reflect and celebrate no specific reference. The hands of an adult,
says he, lie there dazed, a discipline for self-realization. Circling
around an unnamed middle of ready sounds the baby is thrown
off-balance though hopefully not through the window, as once
happened to moi. Or the sound of a fretless bass. Play it again,
but with more *mwah* this time. In practice the baby becomes
more and more expansive; with others no diaper fits. I had
a job teaching about the experience of being a baby, something
I know nothing about, says he. I've never been asked this
question until now, says he, therefore it is sometimes painful.
But if steering a car were to consist of nothing but musical signals
made exits the turn of the baby lying in wait at the off-ramp
will take a little re-editing. An audience for that might also be
a little protective about it, though it's hard to imagine.

Our World in the Baby's Mind

The unemployed lost in war, choice of gray glass through black air,
between egalitarian settlements of location one building and the next
transformed in false ideals, feelings, the whole psychosis outside itself.
The idea of no existence in commencement, dropping a recipient's
objectivity in ruin, in the soul train; the virtual context, bedded, bathes.
Cups of coffee in thoughts dismayed, disengaged, drifting, invalidated,
getting stronger. The best part of a severed tongue in the bottom
toward perfect error proves pleasure's awkward clay, the dish of time
and space, an adjacency on demand, impermanent, rarely functioning.
The stars of the night dissolve a suicidal campaign soldiering the
smokescreen, a necklace torn to pieces, fortunes climbing
conventional forms and new forms, everything hidden, crossing or
by the bulges, folds, crevices, jagged textures. The rock walls,
the limits. The limits do not stay, will not stay still. A substitution,
a fake potato vomit in a liquid heaven. Baked beans bacon teaspoon
concerto, brain bent on the black tree. Lime-green phoneme,
unbearable muffin, indefinite bliss. An old-fashioned sandal,
clothesline, the letter b of body a problem patron. In soft distances,
lank pages of the book, in language of this water in letters
somber alphabets fallen; graceful curves, reflected images, woody.
Cruel twin pools pee in britches, reflect that material pleasure,
dimension's outer light on bended knee cigarette in their
small damp stones. A perfectly level purchase, halls of money,
all farewell, that stored math grazing a receding wave. Repairing it,
saying goodbye. Opening the instrument, the performance.

Taste a White Undershirt, Minty and Lemony
to Trace Peterson

In one's mouth, splash against the side of the bucket.
Fall prey, promise. With no home in this world anymore,
keep up the pace—almost run. Each on his quest intent,
in endless procession they pass, tragic, grotesque, gay,
they all sweep onward like rain falling upon leaves. I wonder
where they are going. What will happen? Defaunate cryptic
phenomenon, end up with the non-cryptic functioning.
Be like Lebanon, grape leaves on a tray and then they're gone,
spot on the sun departs toward heaven. Escape from imitate
from tall trees sip, sharpen bone. Replace the doorway,
clarify and deepen devotion to language and style, dissolve
personality all the way back. Think about extinction to pay
attention to a pile of mud. Play a central role that all
the declarations are divested of, then work out the vocabulary
of what will be opened. Love the onset of the horror
streaming with losts and founds, adjust the enjoyment of it
between them, fill this loveliness in a watery rave. Taste
one more round calculated to contain a justifiable outrage
decision-makers advise, including the little hierarchies
one had to dismantle. The drinks that burn more slender
accents in porcelain purchase connote in a meter every tree
has set on its head. Tomorrow an unwholesome literature,
uninjurable and unchangeable, squirts ooze from its
unhesitatingly plump cod, broad-minded and fair, whipped
by the devil to withdraw its purities from the pollution
before it is entirely spent. It seems like a lot of work.
Life and death use this to spice up your love life, obviously
'the social' is inaccessible to a tree limb.

Some Say
to Ruth Danon

The identity of every culture always lies
at the frontiers, the remnant disintegrating
the true place where God chooses to dwell
outsourcing human beings. Some say, my knees
caught fire. Others, an incomparable hand
shaken unearths the stock assimilations to
the impetus of patrimony, none a holy need
hiddenmost of spirit, morningless eating late
at night, and not eating less, the hot in the basin
was not coherent. Spilt onto a sheet of paper
immortality involves even pulpier pleasure
from the body parts of persons under attack.
The lone workman, a short, sturdy fellow
named Paco, tormenting the demon who
dwells in the forest, climbs out of the window
moved by the sunset he was watching, his
flashlight swishing the half darkness in search
of its meaning, its continuance. In paradise
one won't be afraid of the incomprehensible
rhythm, the immediacy of ice shelves, submission
to injustice, material pleasure in a sentimental
image for romance. Substance takes sustenance
in stored match strobe rioting flowcharts, from
guardhouse echoes cross the science purrs.
Product a functioning revolver sprints back
with bullets every pincushion minus a left eye.
But all reflections aren't Arendt or penetrate
fixed tissue. An attunement in opposite tensions
two dozen men kill the engine, take a look on foot.

Plascic

to John Shoptaw

First and last, as many times as necessary, homogenized
into complexity, conformity, and weakness the Polar Bear,
that dear friend, and of course Nemo, ranging always from his
anemone and coral bed observe what happens to
the exploitation they jeopardize – where they may frolic
at their ease, in freedom – when it is confused with the void
to the point where a series of traps for the capture of objects
too proud for the farce of giving and receiving, as occasion
requires, of great technical gifts and variety remarks on
space and possessiveness where all possession is dissolved.
Plastic pollution from the present to the future owed neither
to nature or to a technical ability plunges into the vain
contemplation of God whose account of it does not
get into corporeality but rather to the loss of contemplation
in a way that turns the plastic into something like the pure
and absolute medium of pollution in the mind of God
or of man, neither a real logical bottle nor a real pollutant.
That is why nothing about plastic or pollution can be
conceived of as certain or stable. Hence the unique fascination
that plastic exercises over the human mind. Nevertheless,
plastic is not separate from the pollution: it is the thing itself.
At the end of the lane plastic sandals make comical
squelching noises, water oozing from the little diamond-shaped
holes on the top of the sandals. Freedom and bondage
are the most effective means of seduction? It's almost
as if they let it slip that we are the arch polluters
with no feeling whatsoever for pollution. In America,
if something can't be measured it doesn't exist. What I mean
is, many don't work with the impossibility of ever
reaching the truth. The problem of plastic is its vocabulary
isn't more involved with its own meaning.

Acknowledgments

But these are my own reflections, and I am by no means sure that I am right in attributing them to the gross impropriety of a man's betting his brains like bank-notes. Gliding down a staircase with a champagne glass in my hand, I no longer argue with talent. Social scientists run a special kind of risk, because their work does seem, superficially, to share certain goals with the ideological generalizers. Researchers have to be extra-careful to ensure that the biases and preconceptions of the political space don't bleed into their work. And they have to be sober and realistic about the conclusions they draw from their research. Additionally, it might not hurt to make sure that your methods are something other than totally shitty. The choice to constellate certain kinds of rituals, stories, propositions and epistemological modes into a single package called "religion" is a fairly recent, European, and Protestant phenomenon. Similarly, the idea that religiousness is separable from the rest of culture, in such a way that you can see it quantifiably motivating certain behaviors, would seem alien and weird to a lot of people, for whom Faith is not so easily distinguished from other strands of culture. The world is being ruled by doubles under my command: ALAN DAVIES IS THE ONLY LANGUAGE POET WHO HAS EVER HAD SEX. I like the formal work of these pieces, the way they mimic our overloaded information age in order to subvert the depoliticization intrinsic in those news-on-the-go forms. The majority of the other reader's work I might characterize as "young," one wrote on an imaginary girlfriend in an Adam Sandler mode, a young woman poet exhibited her flirty sexuality, and a knucklehead had poems about hanging out with the moneyed set in the Hamptons – idiotically horrible, in every way. As Tonya pointed out, he thought he was Wordsworth, or something, escaping the "stink" of the city.

If you find the poems dark, let me know. I'm considering sending them to *The Nation* from Derek Walcott.

"I think fragments of glass had pierced his head," she recounts. "His face was a mess because of the blood flowing from his head. But he looked at my face and smiled. His smile has remained glued in my memory." Aliends and psychonauts vis-a-vis DMT. There are so many surprises in the poem, including the entrance of Paco, whose entrance reminds me of the surprise entrance of Ramon Hernandez in "The Idea of Order at Key West."

But should taxpayers have to pay for that discrimination? Thomas Jefferson would turn in his grave. I've got a house by the roadside made out of rattlesnake skin. You know it's made from a human skull. Who do you love?

It's just blowing my mind that despite an element of anti-technology in hippiedom there were enough that were driven to put computers in the hands of The People and snatch the Internet from ARPA and make it possible for so many to see and hear such performances that surely would have been seen only by a select few, especially if some bean counter decided it had "no commercial value." Long live Peace, Love, Truth and Creativity!

100% with you, this goes beyond passion, it is a cosmic orgasm.

I'd forgotten what it felt like being in the woods, so to speak. The first night I slept like a baby and enjoyed the most lucid and lengthy narrative-like dreams. It may have been that my body relaxed from the tensions of travel between NJ and NYC and breathed the air of the Berkshires deep into my lungs. So it may take a while, but I'm preparing to prioritize reading this stuff. It is an almost hopeless task, for there is rarely a day when at some time the dust clouds do not roll over and everything is covered again with a silt-like deposit which may vary in depth from a film to actual ripples on the kitchen floor. I keep oiled cloths on the windowsills and between the upper and lower sashes. They help just a little to retard or collect the dust. . . .

Thanks.

Finale

Wrap-Around Comb-Over

Chair-lined corridors are riddled with Gulliver and Lilliputians strangely
Unconcerned with interdepartmental squabbles. Dangerous people
Hold wrong views from ignorance (some think) making more enemies
Every time they act. Subjectivity is a sort of tautology; you see how sad
The American landscape is today. The supreme points in its evolution,
Spiritually and culturally as well as politically, permeate the genuine artist
Afraid to call for the simplest chord. The original celestial character of
This fundamental is the constitution of subjectivity's limits. The possibility
Of settling its bureaucrats with meaningfully productive labor is
Considered a kind of defiance by the 'divine government', the same
Specter that for lack of love asks nothing but at the same time does
Everything possible in order for it to be forgotten. Correspondingly,
The manifestoization in the acceleration of the news pauses to weaken
The laws restricting gun purchases. One can be taxing and hazardous, but
Never dull. Expunged without physically damaging the underlying surface,
Rotting away other-oriented economies might appear arbitrary.
The dividend of immateriality though seeming chimerical or nonexistent
Is the end product of long traditions and trajectories of unpronounceable
Good faith efforts. Centers of calculation, overtly immaterial and
Idealized, have one coughing and spluttering. Sundry constellations dis-
Incentivize learned councilors and other officials' resistance as the best means
Of infiltrating friends and family waiting to cultivate ancestral lands. Suspicion
Exists in the chauffeur's tact. If memory serves, polite incomprehension
Stabilizes ascendants. Surveillance in one's pocket implants a micro-eye
Of ideological war. Wittgenstein should wield a sword. An old prosperity
From the new way of life recuperates a false decorum, and friends.
The scented life of culture czars whose talents are sporadic, eager to attack
And rapidly exhausted, is intolerant of discursive amplification except
When contrived to exhaust the inessential.

In the Presence of one's Enemies

A sign of reactionary recrudescence's rim shot
representative of the theater for salutary clownish mirth,
its blatant disgracefulnesses that signify the culture
of the age, an on holiday ruthlessness genomed down
for the tourists on a synthetic melon asking revelers
resurfacing the oval square with pre-skirmish thinkers
high on petrol, real-time maps, anorexia, and programmable
Alzheimer's and drugs to cure them, explains
as understatement anything and everything
between brilliance and murk. For the intelligent
there is only one landscape, its calm and finality
is an extremely rare one. In this intensified, turned-on
state each solitary writing session sounds and silences
tentacle-like primitive living things manipulating
and massaging little diamond-shaped holes
half-covered in a tangle of roots pre-ordained
to the jam jar the rope ladder by God, an Edenic
sexuality under the clothes of grace even more obscene
than the indolence of shaved nuts expiates ecological
dilemmas. Almost hard to see the old obstacle in the road.
An indispensable in the heavenly plane boasts
a particular quickness whereby terminological pretensions
browbeat, black with printer's ink, justice. Intimidated
to be in a family modern quotas on far-off Fuji
accept corporate monoliths and landmarks: lotus roots
big as babies buy a styro of Starbucks and an aqua.
Hoarding one's environment is a key to one's identity;
friends *crawl* with jealousy.

When you're Still Sleeping

When you're sleeping, the mind responds to your expectations,
And to the script you bring to it, but art does not reflect
Your beliefs back to you, nor allow us to penetrate this Platonic
World. But I can't get rid of the doubt that it is the world's most
Powerful placebo. Children sleep, when they can, without
Their parents. In an invisible aether, complicated mathematical gymnastics
Are needed to remove infinities toward a horizontal transcendence,
Rather than a vertical individualist transcendence. It enables a minuscule
Bubble of space to burst into being from nothing, to then inflate
To astronomical scales the weapons of white supremacy. I remain contemptuous
Of creamed herring. Speaking of divine Nothingness, a twenty-minute
Intermission was just announced. Patterns of abuse have promulgated
A transparency that leaves so much out the web moves in its sleep
To twitter handles pimping power to the finance data sanctuaries
Destroyed in its proximity. The unfitness of the poem suits me quite well.
Fragments of light, interstellar dumplings, clip what one watches.
In the realm of rubber ruddy Lilliputians run about riddled with religion
And politics, but it doesn't seem their skill with rope dancing
Can say definitively. The souls of their feet fill the entire universe;
Something the mouth cannot express, nor the ear hear. Our irregular
Durations, e.g., lives, prevent one's memory from registering
Convergence and de-convergence; passwords to the coming world.
This poem is not about El Paso. The story at the terrorism checkout
Counter is too long. We've never been so scared in our lives.

Everyone is Your Home
with help from Celan

When it's stated that "in terms of access, telematics replaces the doorway,"
I wish I could use the bathroom without opening the door. It's real meat and
Vegetables, and the lie is in you. Instead of spreading goodwill, you pimp for it.
Poetry makes it impossible to reuse the American people. These people
Have no heart. These people (or what lies on them) are circulating in our
Communities. I may be infected with the minds of the American people. With
The moral dysentery, massage parlors, and bowling alleys. On the ground,
Liver inflamed on ultrasound, buying gluten-free, twelve hour shits, parked
On a couch lymph nodes swollen with concern, grit in teeth. Farmers
Plowing under their crops. Antifreeze in their drinking water. In light
Of that, everyone shares the same body. The filters and the mind are
Propaganda. Autobiographical recollections? From specks to mountains
Something's wrong. It is comforting to think that the disproportion of things
In the world seems to be only arithmetical. An injured vanity, a good
Florida grapefruit, a kind of martial law connecting consumers and the light
On the grotesquely grimacing retreating face. Like they say, someone
Needs to be held. This is the poem I am writing to you. Shouldn't you
Do something similar? What one only partially understands is in principle
Incompossible, snug as a bug in a rug. Nickle and dimed it just shatters.
Your faith in people? The oracle's next mission is clarified and deepened to
Support Americans in their spiritual obsoleteness. A sip and it's off
To dreamland. "In night's friable matter." Take a listen: In the vertical
Narrow daygorge something came to stand. Where does it stand?

Slave Patrols and Night Watches
365 days a year George Floyd

All guns are smoking. There are enough to stock
A miniseries. Your pain is real. It is perhaps my immaturity,
Now and then, i.e., relatively seldom, that prompts the
Realization that my activities are superior to me. The known
And unknown aided and abetted. What was in their minds?
Surveys are helpless. Instantaneous propaganda-makers,
And the intensity of it, need to be studied. Premeditation
Assumes peasants are uninformed. Errors proliferate
Without end. Even helicopters demand change. In a vague
Ritual gesture, unsold seats take advantage of giveaways to
Indifference. It guarantees the people trying to get on
Are fighting with those who are trying to get off. Faraway
Places disappear. The nebula coheres. "What am I to do with
Lamentation?" What is your hospital capacity? I'm fourth
Generation airless. Spiritual clarities provide illness and death.
Postscript? Patriarchs prey on the stage of our depraved
Interlude, pure products of America gone crazy. Purveyors of
An alien calculus, it's not possible to avoid killing.

Not a Day without a Lie

The minimalism, formalism and indeterminism make it a harbinger
Of crickets or the patter of rain, of so much to come. We know nothing
Of the invisible, or of veal cooked in cream. Faraway places disappear.
The specific mutation targets the eyes of the world. Wuhan to
Washington. Curb-side rentals and transactions are wholly imperceptible
To those imprisoned by them. Seamlessly, the lives of savages or
A less discernible irony has completely deserted the real. Whistling
Dixie, whether one wanted to or not, the prestige of personal existence,
Its impotence and entanglement committed to optical illusions, a
Comfortless distance of imbecility, is complete. All guns are smoking.
You enter their breath with limitless trust. In drifting snowflakes one
Gropes toward sugar or almonds, raisons, or preserves unencumbered by
Bread. The capitol of a primeval frenzy achieved by particular mixtures
Of memorable aphorisms and precious bodily fluids. The old
Narratives, sleeping cars to eternity, are consulted. In the biggest closet
An orange jumpsuit reopens its magical kingdom. On the horizontal
Bar of exclusion, in gentle radiance, shut up and dribble. Due to de-
Funding of bibliomaniacs, scarcity enters life as a stammer (and the trees
Come to their senses). The shaman's soothsaying is occupied by
Family values – the most ordinary of iron gates. 'After great pain,
A formal feeling comes— the Hour of Lead' leads one to feel, while
Trying to crack the code, a little crazy. Welcome back. I'm reminded
Of the words "I can't breathe," and of the bliss of the epileptic.

Synthetic Investments
to Varavara Rao

I just want the baby to disappear, and I'll disappear.
He's such a sweet fellow, but some thugs should change,
amen. Trying to make a final decision this morning
so I can move past this baby exchange idea. Do the
numbers again. I wish I had inherited more diapers.
The draining of the diapers creates another hazard
in the home. As poop is pulled from the spongy diaper,
the air above collapses, creating what is known as
subsidence. Where subsidence is the worst, the air can
sink as much as a foot each week. Babies arrive beneath
one's skin. Air scarcity, or tightening belts, have neighboring
babies eyeing one another warily. That's their diversion point.
We're all in this together, but it's every baby for him or her
self. Babies despise asymmetry. They take off their clothes
to transcend embarrassment. Baby says, I'm going to eat
the whole thing. There's only one present to share.
I am nursed by the virtuosity of exceptionalism. A parent
cries out, I don't think we're going to get the antiseptic in time.
Another baby comments, Gotta love humans. They have
such huge assholes. Nice and slow the polluted waters
perform. The baby burns its fingers depleting the warmth
of organic synthesis. Selective cleavage requests the baby's
participation. It makes one wonder where the country is.

171

Additional Acknowledgments

Grateful acknowledgement is made for publishing the poems and prose in *Artifice in the Calm Damages* to Anselm Berrigan at *The Brooklyn Rail*; to Michael Boughn and Kent Johnson at *Dispatches from the Poetry Wars*; to Rebecca Wolff at *Fence*; to Page Delano and Elizabeth Wissinger at *Inquirer*; to Thomas Fink at *Marsh Hawk Review*; to Susan Lewis at *Posit*, to Ed Foster at *Talisman*, to Noam Scheindlin at *Warscapes*; to Manuel Brito at Zasterle Press for work in *The Canary Islands Connection – 60 Contemporary American Poets* (Tenerife, Spain); to Mary Newell, Bernard Quetchenbach, and Sarah Nolan, the editors of *Poetics-for-the-More-than-Human-World – An Anthology of Poetry & Commentary*; and to the Dispatches Editions editors of *Resist Much / Obey Little – Inaugural Poems to the Resistance*. Much love to Norman Fischer for "Condemnation, confrontation, remembrance," a conversation on *Artifice in the Calm Damages* at *Jacket2*; to Leila Rosner for an exchange on *Artifice* published at Tom Fink's *Dichtung Yammer*; to Marta Lopez-Luaces for translating several poems into Spanish for the *Bilingual Poetry Series*, *Readings @ Tompkins*; to Anne Noonan for a lovely letterpress broadside of "A Great Blue Wet World of Thought" presented in a performance with Norman Fischer & Jascha Hoffman at The Shed, Brooklyn; to Charles Alexander and Cynthia Miller for the beautiful chapbook in 2017; and to Sadie who has shown me how to find one's soul in the art of scratching.

Special thanks to Ammiel Alcalay, Joe Amato, Jennifer Bartlett, Steve Benson, Charles Borkhuis, Michael Boughn, Abigail Child, Margie Cronin, Ruth Danon, Jean Day, Thom Donovan, Patrick Dunagan, Daria Fain, Norman Fischer, Drew Gardener, Paolo Javier, Kent Johnson, Burt Kimmelman, Robert Kocik, Susan Lewis, Miriam Nichols, Julie Patton, Ted Pearson, Jesse Seldess, John Shoptaw, André Spears, Eleni Stecopoulos, Sharon Thesen, and Tyrone Williams, for their keen eyes and ears and for their assistance on what to do with *Artifice in the Calm Damages*.

About the Author

Andrew Levy is the author of *Notes toward a Supreme Fiction 2029*, *Artifice in the Calm Damages* (chapbook), *Don't Forget to Breathe*, *Nothing Is in Here* (novella), and ten other collections of poetry and prose. His poems and essays have appeared in numerous American and international magazines and anthologies, including *Poetics-for-the-More-than-Human-World – An Anthology of Poetry & Commentary*; *Light Abstracts the Smallest Things: The Aesthetics of Basil King*; *The Canary Islands Connection – 60 Contemporary American Poets*; and *Resist Much / Obey Little – Inaugural Poems to The Resistance*. Levy's writing works on the intersections of class and the ecology of commerce, and experimental music and the digitalization of freedom. A drummer, he works in collaboration with musicians and poets on readings and performances. He teaches journalism at BMCC-CUNY.

About Chax

Founded in 1984 in Tucson, Arizona, Chax has published more than 240 books in a variety of formats, including hand printed letterpress books and chapbooks, hybrid chapbooks, book arts editions, and trade paperback editions such as the book you are holding. From August 2014 until July 2018 Chax Press resided in Houston-Victoria Center for the Arts. Chax is a nonprofit 501(c)(3) organization which depends on suppport from various government & private funders, and, primarly, from individual donors and readers. In July 2018 Chax Press returned to Tucson, Arizona, while maintaining some affiliation with the University of Houston-Victoria. Our current address is 1517 North Wilmot Road no. 264, Tucson, Arizona 85712-4410. You can email us at *chaxpress@chax.org*

You may find CHAX at *https://chax.org*